Joseph S. Nicholson

Tenant's Gain Not Landlord's Loss

And some other economic aspects of the land question

Joseph S. Nicholson

Tenant's Gain Not Landlord's Loss
And some other economic aspects of the land question

ISBN/EAN: 9783337312107

Printed in Europe, USA, Canada, Australia, Japan

Cover: Foto ©Suzi / pixelio.de

More available books at **www.hansebooks.com**

TENANT'S GAIN

NOT

LANDLORD'S LOSS

AND SOME OTHER ECONOMIC ASPECTS OF THE LAND QUESTION

BY

JOSEPH SHIELD NICHOLSON, M.A.

PROFESSOR OF COMMERCIAL AND POLITICAL ECONOMY AND MERCANTILE LAW IN THE UNIVERSITY OF EDINBURGH

Come, let us talk a little of the affairs of the nation or some such subject that we can all of us understand.—SQUIRE WESTERN.

EDINBURGH: DAVID DOUGLAS

1883

Cum igitur animum ad Politicam applicuerim, nihil quod novum vel inauditum est, sed tantum ea quæ cum praxi optime conveniunt demonstrare intendi; et ut ea, quæ ad hanc scientiam spectant, eadem animi libertate, qua res Mathematicas solemus, inquirerem, sedulo curavi humanas actiones non ridere, non lugere, neque detestari, sed intelligere.—SPINOZA.

PREFACE.

My apology for adding to the number of books on the Land Question is the hope that the application of some leading principles of Political Economy to the subject may be of service. Although constant references are made to the principles of that science, it is very rarely that a writer or a speaker condescends to details, and yet it can hardly be doubted that the labours of Adam Smith and his successors (and no subject has a wider literature than Political Economy) have done something towards the solution of the difficult problems connected with land. The vitality of popular fallacies is remarkable, and the old mercantile notion of trade that one man's gain is necessarily another man's loss still prevails as regards compensation for agricultural improvements. The exposure of this and other fallacies is one of the principal aims of this volume; but, at the same time, I have attempted to contribute something positive to the controversy, by suggesting the abandonment of the time-honoured division of improvements' into "permanent" and "temporary," and the adoption of a more logical and important ground of distinction.[1] I have also ventured to express my own opinion on other matters of practical importance, and I hope that the statement of principles generally accepted by economists will not lose in force on account of deductions for which I must take the whole responsibility. I have to express my great obligation to Mr. Henry H. Scott, Alnham House, Alnwick, for his kind assistance in the more practical parts of the work, and to Mr. W. C. Smith, Advocate, for suggestions and corrections as the book was going through the Press.

J. S. N.

THE UNIVERSITY, EDINBURGH,
11*th May* 1883.

[1] *Cf.* Chap. x.

CONTENTS.

CHAPTER I.

The Place of Agriculture in the Industrial System.

CHAPTER II.

On the Principles and Objects of Legislation in regard to Land.

CHAPTER III.

On the Economic Results of a Simple System of Transfer of Property in Land.

CHAPTER IV.

The Law of Diminishing Return to Land.

CHAPTER V.

Malthus and the Crofters.

CHAPTER VI.

Ricardo's Theory of Rent.

CHAPTER VII.

The Nationalisation of Land.

CHAPTER VIII.

The Causes which Determine the Fair Rent of Land.

CHAPTER IX.

CHAPTER X.

CHAPTER XI.

THE RIGHTS OF PROPERTY, AND THE RIGHTS OF LABOUR.

CHAPTER XII.

ON THE PROBABLE APPRECIATION OF GOLD AND CYCLES OF INFLATION AND DEPRESSION OF TRADE.

CHAPTER XIII.

CONCLUSION.

CHAPTER I.

THE PLACE OF AGRICULTURE IN THE INDUSTRIAL SYSTEM.

"In agriculture Nature labours along with man, and though her labour costs no expense, its produce has its value as well as that of the most expensive workmen."

ADAM SMITH.

PROBABLY in most countries agriculture is the most important of all industries, and certainly it is the most important industry of the United Kingdom. The average value of the gross agricultural produce is greater than the total value of our exports, and notwithstanding the increase in the variety and abundance of valuable commodities consequent on the advance of civilisation, the value of the land of the United Kingdom is almost a fourth of its estimated aggregate wealth. In Great Britain there are more than 560,000 tenant-farmers, and probably a tenth of the working population is engaged in agriculture.

But the importance of agriculture cannot be thoroughly understood merely from a comparison of industrial statistics. Adam Smith pointed out that no equal employment of labour and capital in manufactures can produce so much wealth as in agriculture, the wealth, of course, being estimated in the only manner which is possible, namely by its value. The ground of this assertion is that capital employed in agriculture yields not only the ordinary rate of profits to the farmer, but over and above a surplus in the shape of rent. Of the fact there can be no doubt, and if the principle on which farmers' profits are assessed for income-tax is just, farmers' profits in England are only one-half the rent, and in Scotland one-third. But although there can be no dispute as to the matter of fact, there has been much controversy as to the proper explanation, and Adam Smith's theory on the subject has been very severely criticised by most writers on economics. That theory, briefly expressed, amounts to this: Nature lends more assistance to human endeavours in agriculture than in manufactures; or, in the extreme and unguarded language of Adam Smith, "in manufactures Nature does nothing." This unfortunate expression has been made the pretext for a good deal of very wise writing on the old text, "E nihilo nihil fit." It has been gravely pointed out by J. S. Mill that "labour in the physical world is always and solely employed in putting objects in motion, the properties of matter, the laws of nature, do the rest;" and he modestly asserts in a note that the discovery of this fundamental principle of political economy is due to the elder Mr. Mill. As a corollary to this principle it is maintained—"It is impossible to decide that in any one thing nature does more than in any other. One cannot even say that labour does less. Less labour may be required, but if that which is required is absolutely indispensable, the result is just as much the product of labour as of nature. When two conditions are equally necessary for producing the effect at all, it is unmeaning to say that so much of it is produced by one and so much by the other; it is like attempting to decide which half of a pair of scissors has most to do in the act of cutting;" or, it might be added, which contributes most to the organ recital, the man at the key-board or the man at the bellows. But, as often happens, an important truth has been neglected, because not clothed in the full dress of accurate scientific phraseology. If we look below the surface, to the ideas that the words stand for, as John Locke would say, it is clear that Adam Smith wished to point out that in the acquisition of certain commodities nature saves man trouble and labour—in some cases indeed (*e.g.* wild fruits) all labour except the mere labour of "occupancy." The distinction may be illustrated by the case of a commodity which at first is only produced artificially, and is afterwards discovered in a natural source (*e.g.* mineral oil). The proposition may also be expressed thus: "To obtain commodities of equal value different quantities of labour are necessary according to natural conditions." It follows immediately that it is for the interest of the society in the first place to appropriate the gifts of nature, and that the natural order of the progress of opulence is from agriculture to manufactures. It is clear, too, taking a society in an advanced state of civilisation, that the most advantageous employment of capital is in agriculture, at least so long as this employment yields a rent. It must not be forgotten that the total rent of a country is part of the surplus agricultural profits, which in the first place means surplus produce. The mere fact that the landlord is the first person to receive the rent does not make it of less national importance. Hence a rise in aggregate rent due to increase in produce by better farming, or to an extension of the land under cultivation, is a greater economic gain than an equal rise in the profits of manufactures. If, as some authorities maintain—or, at any rate, the case may be supposed—the agricultural produce of this country could be doubled, and if the aggregate rent of the country were doubled at the same time, such an event would be more advantageous than if the gross produce of manufactures of equal value were doubled; for the rent obtained in the former case shows that the labour and capital is more advantageously employed, supposing, of course, that the rates of wages and profits are uniform in both cases. It is not necessary to point out that if the rise in rent is due to restrictions on foreign importations, the reasoning does not apply—the argument presupposes a system of natural liberty.

But the relative importance of agriculture to a society is defended by Adam Smith on other grounds. He maintains that capital is more advantageously employed within a society than abroad. It is true the rate of profits on capital, whatever be the mode of its employment, tends to equality, and regard being paid to certain natural causes of differences of profits in different employments, the rate of profits is, in fact, greater in the foreign than in the home trade. But advantage is not synonymous with a high rate of profit. To the labouring classes the rate of profit is a matter of indifference so long as it is sufficient to keep the capital employed, but it is a serious matter to them if capital on a large scale is exported. Again, to the capitalist, it is a matter of indifference whether his capital is sunk in British or in foreign railways so long as he gets the same rate of interest, but it is by no means a matter of indifference to the British public. This extremely important distinction, like so much that is valuable in *The Wealth of Nations*, has been eliminated from modern Political Economy by the hypothetical hypercriticism of Ricardo: "Provided its net real income, its *rents and profits*, be the same, it is of no importance whether the nation consists of ten or of twelve millions of inhabitants. Its power of supporting fleets and armies and all species of unproductive labour must be in proportion to its net, and not to its gross, income." No doubt, by the aid of judicious definitions and hypotheses, this statement may be made verbally true, but in the meantime the important doctrine of Adam Smith has vanished.

But Adam Smith carries his preference for agriculture still further: "The capital, however, that is acquired to any country by commerce and manufactures is all a very precarious and uncertain possession, till some part of it has been secured and realised in the cultivation and improvement of its lands. A merchant, it has been said very properly, is not necessarily the citizen of any particular country. It is in a great measure indifferent to him from what place he carries on his trade; and a very trifling disgust will make him remove his capital, and together with it all the industry which it supports from one country to another. No part of it can be said to belong to any particular country till it has been spread, as it were, over the face of that country either in buildings, or in the lasting improvements of lands. No vestige now remains of the great wealth said to have been possessed by the greater part of the Hanse towns, except in the obscure histories of the thirteenth and fourteenth centuries. . . . That which arises from the more solid improvements of agriculture is much more durable, and cannot be destroyed but by those more violent convulsions occasioned by the depredations of hostile and barbarous nations continued for a century or two together; such as those that happened for some time after the fall of the Roman empire, in the western provinces of Europe."[1]

[1] Adam Smith's *Wealth of Nations*, Book iii. chap. iv.

CHAPTER II.

ON THE PRINCIPLES AND OBJECTS OF LEGISLATION IN REGARD TO LAND.

"Laws frequently continue in force long after the circumstances which first gave occasion to them, and which could alone render them reasonable, are no more."

ADAM SMITH.

THE conflict of opinions on the expediency and objects of legislation in regard to land arises to a great extent from diverging views on the general principles of legitimate Government interference. Notwithstanding all the efforts of Adam Smith and his followers, the opinion still largely obtains that Government can do anything, and that everything it does will be much better done than by individuals. It is assumed, for instance, that a Government official will fix a fairer rent than would emerge from free contract, and that the valuation of improvements can be just only when officially carried out. The appointment of Land Commissioners in Ireland, and in fact the whole tenor of the Irish Land Act, has strengthened the presumption. People have begun to suspect that those who cry loudest will get most of the Government cake, and a perfect Babel of cries has of late been raised for Government help and interference in all directions, and especially on behalf of our depressed agriculture. It is not superfluous then to point out that, according to the teaching of the best English political economists, the presumption is always against Government interference, and unless a strong case is made out to the contrary, in favour of *laisser faire.* The reasons in support of this position are the commonplaces of English political economy,[1] and it is sufficient to recall the facts that Government has already too much to do, that self-interest is the greatest incentive to industry, and that people know their own interests better and can look after them better than the most paternal of Governments. The doctrine of *laisser faire* has in recent times obtained a more scientific basis in the theory of development, a theory which has revolutionised the study of history, whether social, economic, or legal. It is now clearly seen that the mere antiquity of an institution is no proof of its expediency in the modern world—it may be simply a survival from the past, a functionless organ that is only an encumbrance. It is seen that a society is progressive in proportion as it casts off the laws, customs, and institutions which are not adapted to its new environment, and substitutes those which

[1] *Cf.* Mill, bk. v. ch. ii.

are. In the words of Sir Henry Maine, which have become proverbial, "The progress of society has been from *status* to contract," from Government interference to *laisser faire.* "Legislation has nearly confessed its inability to keep pace with the activity of man in discovery, in invention, and in the manipulation of accumulated wealth; and the law, even of the least advanced communities, tends more and more to become a mere surface stream, having under it an ever-changing assemblage of contractual rules, with which it rarely interferes except to compel compliance with a few fundamental principles, or unless it be called on to punish the violation of good faith."[1] No doubt the Government of every civilised society has continually to perform new functions, but the necessity arises from new conditions, and it is an error to suppose that the proportion of work done by Government for the individual members of society, compared with the work they do for themselves, is on the increase. Freedom of action in the individual is essential to economic as to all other development; if Government, at the close of last century, had listened to the appeal of the distressed operatives to fix wages and to keep in force the old customs by which competition was restricted and stability of employment secured, the system of large industries would have been strangled in its birth. It is only by allowing individuals the greatest pos-

[1] *Ancient Law*, p. 305.

sible freedom for experiments that the best type can be obtained.

But although both history and theory point to *laisser faire* as the general rule for progressive societies, certain important exceptions of wide range have come to be recognised as expedient; for example, on the ground that the consumer is not always a competent judge of the commodity purchased,[1] laws forbidding the adulteration of goods and rendering the education of children compulsory have met with general approval, and the principle on which the limitation of the hours of labour rests may be at once instanced as having an important bearing on the relations of landlord and tenant. "There are matters," says Mill, "in which the interference of law is required, not to override the judgment of individuals respecting their own interest, but to give effect to that judgment; they being unable to give effect to it except by concert, which concert, again, cannot be effectual unless it receives validity and sanction from the law."[2] The Commissioners on Agriculture report that in many cases landlords have omitted to offer and tenants to ask for compensation, and yet compensation to some extent is generally considered to be advantageous by both parties. But what average tenant will insist on compensation when he knows another will take the farm without it? and what average landlord will give up a proprietary right

[1] *Cf.* Mill, bk. v. ch. xi. sect. 8. [2] *Ibid.* sect. 12.

which his neighbour still retains? The list of recognised exceptions to *laisser faire* might easily be extended; suffice it to mention the cases where the contracting parties are not on an equal footing, as in the case of monopolies, and where certain contracts are supposed to be injurious to health, life, or morality (witness the long series of Factory Acts). Although, then, the political economy built on English lines—on the lines laid down by Adam Smith—makes *laisser faire* its fundamental principle, still it allows such large exceptions that we can never say *primâ facie*, in any particular case, that Government interference is not desirable.

It is necessary, then, at the outset, to consider what objects Government should have in view if it is to interfere with the distribution of land or with the relations of landlord and tenant; for much of the confusion of the present controversy arises from the various and even contradictory aims which different sections of the community wish the Government to adopt, and the only way to reduce the chaos to anything like order seems to be to make clear and explicit what is in general confused and implied, and to set sharply before the advocates of reforms on the one hand, and the conservators of "a vast system of law" on the other, the various principles to which they tacitly appeal. It is useless to demand legislation, whether destructive or constructive, until the goal of legislation is clearly defined; and even if the opposing parties are so evenly balanced that no practical result is attainable, it is still useful to have the points in dispute sharply stated.

(1.) First of all, then, there are those who insist on the sacred rights of property, and who think the object of Government should be to make property in land as absolute as the nature of the case will permit. They regard with peculiar horror anything of the nature of tenant right, and are often heard to say that "a bargain is a bargain." They see very clearly the rights, but very imperfectly the duties, of landlords. They fear the introduction of the thin end of the socialistic wedge, and are loud in their praises of the political economy of individualism. Now, there is certainly a considerable amount of practical wisdom evinced in the adoption of this attitude; it is a dangerous thing, with socialism rampant on the Continent, to interfere with any kind of private property, and it is only playing with words to say that the recent Irish legislation was not socialistic[1] in its tendency—of which the constant reiteration of "thus far shalt thou go and no further" is sufficient proof. Private property—including private property in land—is one of the most important corner-stones of the social edifice.

Accordingly economists, and Mill especially, whilst insisting on the right of the State to take over any

[1] The essence of all socialistic schemes is to substitute Government control for the competition of individuals.

form of property, if it is deemed expedient, insist at the same time on the necessity for full compensation, even including something of the nature of a *pretium affectionis* to the expropriated proprietors; in fact, of such importance is the institution of private property considered to be, that (apart from taxation) it may be taken as a maxim that any change in property instituted by Government ought to be a change in kind only and not in value, and the doctrine of compensation finds far more support in English political economy than the representatives of English taxpayers seem prepared to admit. At the same time the institution of private property itself only rests upon expediency; there is nothing in Socialism that is necessarily either immoral or unnatural tried by the current morality; from Plato downwards forms of Socialism have commended themselves to some of the brightest and best minds; and the real argument against Utopias is—not that they are immoral, but impracticable. Accordingly, if any limitation of proprietary rights be proposed, the question to be asked is—Is it expedient, and can it be carried into effect? To take an extreme instance: If the owners of land were to extend deer forests over the whole of Scotland on the ground that they had a right to do as they liked with their own, they would soon find that "own" was capable of a very different interpretation.

(2.) Secondly, there are those who raise the cry of "the land for the people:" they are given to regarding the present owners of land as the original plunderers of the nation; they are apt to forget that land changes hands, and to ignore titles by prescription; they seem to think the present landowners the only class in the community who have gained unearned increments at the expense of the masses; they assert that land is not the result of labour, and that labour alone is the equitable basis of private property. They differ in the positive interpretation of the phrase "land for the people," although agreeing in the negative position that land ought not to belong to the present owners. Some who raise the cry appear to think the people would own the land if a considerable number of peasant proprietors were created, whilst others would only be satisfied if Government were made the sole landowner. In both proposals, which, it may be remarked, are logically contradictory, metaphysical arguments founded on "natural" rights are largely used to support or conceal the weakness of the case as resting on expediency. (*Cf.* Ch. XI.) But, taking a lower ground, there are no doubt many economic advantages in the peasant proprietary system: the peasant proprietor is frugal, industrious, and thrifty; although he lives poorly, the consciousness of ownership and the certainty of a livelihood if he acts prudently (supposing climatic conditions are tolerably equable), must always be a source of happiness to him, and ought to promote a manly independence. But it is not often the advocates of the system take the trouble to examine recent evidence, and to compare the actual condition and prospects of the agricultural labourer in this country with that of the peasant owner abroad, and in thinking on the advantages of absolute fixity of tenure they forget those of mobility of labour. Again, it is one thing for peasant proprietors to be created from below by the efforts and sacrifices of agricultural labourers; it is quite another for the *morcellement* to be accomplished by the carving-knife of a paternal Government. At the same time, although it may be doubted whether the expediency of the system founded on an extended scale by direct Government intervention (in Great Britain) could ever be proved to the satisfaction of a British Parliament, the actual difficulties placed in the way of ownership on a small scale are not defensible, unless the system can be shown to be positively injurious to the nation, or the opposite system of large ownership to possess far superior advantages. The Nationalisation of land will be discussed in a separate chapter. (Ch. VII.)

(3.) Thirdly, there are those who regard the question entirely as one of gross production: they profess their complete indifference to forms of ownership and forms of tenure, provided the agricultural produce attains a maximum, and the system of laws which tends to give this maximum is, in their opinion, *ipso facto*, the best. These are the people who think the essence of practical wisdom is embodied in the aphorism on the man who makes two blades of grass grow where one grew before. They are strong in support of large farms and high farming, and clamour for the abolition of game laws and deer forests. They are apt to regard high wages as an evil, because cultivation is checked, and they look askance on the importation of foreign corn and cattle. They whisper amongst themselves that if protection would extend the margin of cultivation or prevent its retrogression, protection is to be desired. But if the man who doubles the blades of grass in a country is a national benefactor, by analogy the same praise must be bestowed on him who doubles the amount of cloth, stockings, lace, and all the varied products of a nation's industrial efforts. But the industrial power of every country is limited by the amount and efficiency of its labour and capital, and if by manufacturing cotton goods we can import more corn than we could grow at the same expense, the two blades of grass theory falls to the ground as far as production is concerned. Under a system of freedom of industry, capital and labour, so far as production is concerned, tend to be employed in the most economic manner, and it is at least possible that the proprietor or farmer who turns moor-land into arable would have employed his share of the national capital to better purpose if he had lent it to a cotton spinner, or taken a share in a ship. It is quite clear that, so far as production is concerned, and apart from considerations of social stability and national defence, protection to agriculture might indeed increase the gross produce, but it could only do so by a waste of national energy. But conversely any artificial restrictions within the country (*e.g.*, preferential laws in favour of owners as against cultivators of the soil) which prevent the gross production attaining its natural limit, ought to be abolished.

(4.) The contention that Government should aim at obtaining a maximum gross produce from the soil, is generally united with the argument that every nation ought to aim at producing its own food supplies on the grounds of political independence and commercial stability. I cannot do better than present this view in the words of Malthus:[1] "Territories of a certain extent must ultimately in the main support their own population. As each exporting country approaches towards that complement of wealth and population to which it is naturally tending, it will gradually withdraw the corn which for a time it had spared to its more manufacturing and commercial neighbours, and leave them to subsist on their own resources. The peculiar products of each soil and climate are objects of foreign trade, which can never under any circumstances fail. But food is not a peculiar product; and the country

[1] *Essay on Population*, bk. iii. ch. xii.

which produces it in the greatest abundance may, according to the laws which govern population, have nothing to spare for others. An extensive foreign trade in corn, beyond what arises from the variableness of the seasons in different countries, is rather a temporary and incidental trade, depending chiefly upon the different stages of improvement which different countries may have reached, and on other accidental circumstances, than a trade which is in its nature permanent, and the stimulus to which will remain in the progress of society unabated. In the wildness of speculation it has been suggested (of course more in jest than in earnest) that Europe ought to grow its corn in America, and devote itself solely to manufactures and commerce as the best sort of division of labour of the globe. But even on the extravagant supposition that the natural course of things might lead to such a division of labour for a time, and that by such means Europe could raise a population greater than its lands could possibly support, the consequences ought to be justly dreaded. It is an unquestionable truth that it must answer to every territorial state, in its natural progress to wealth, to manufacture for itself, unless the countries from which it had purchased its manufactures possess some advantages peculiar to them besides capital and skill. But when upon this principle America began to withdraw its corn from Europe, and the agricultural exertions of Europe were inadequate to make up the deficiency, it would certainly be felt that the temporary advantages of a greater degree of wealth and population (supposing them to have been really attained) had been very dearly purchased by a long period of retrograde movements and misery." On this very remarkable passage by the economist who ranks, perhaps, next to Adam Smith, it may be observed that the dangers indicated seem to be rather political than economic. If free trade prevailed all over the world, the price of corn in America, or any other new country, could never exceed the price in Europe by more than the cost of carriage of the corn and of the export sent to pay for it. But if the new countries imposed restrictions on exportations the old countries might be compelled to pay the whole of a very considerable tax, the inevitable result of which must be a "long period of retrograde movements and misery."

(5.) The supporters of the maximum production ideal generally insist also on the social and economic advantages of a large rural population; they are the sons of the prophets who opposed free trade on the ground that the agricultural labourer is as superior to the factory operative as the squire is to the manufacturer—the superiority in both cases being supposed considerable. It is true that the authority of Adam Smith can be brought forward in favour of this view, and that the social and economic advantages of a due balance between the town and country populations are very great; but at the same time it must be allowed that those who deplore the increase of the town population at the expense of the rural seem to be under the impression that the life of the working classes in towns is, in the words of Hobbes, describing the life of men in a state of nature, "miserable, poor, nasty, brutish, and short;" that it is of necessity so, and that it cannot be ameliorated. The voluntary immigration to the towns from the country, although agricultural wages are rising, shows that those most concerned do not take this gloomy view; and there appears to be as much effeminacy as exaggeration in the lamentation raised over the growth of large manufacturing industries, and the decay of the small system of cultivation. To divide a country into lots, each sufficient to support a happy peasant, does not appear a very attractive ideal; and although the innocence and pleasures of a country life have always called forth praise, most of the working classes find life in a town at any rate tolerable;—the working classes are not to be confounded with paupers, nor are they all the tailors of *Alton Locke*.

Still it is true that, in many cases, the people have been driven from the country to the towns by causes which do not form part of a "natural" system of social economy. Again, although hygienic conditions are more looked after in towns than in the country, there is no doubt that density of population leads to a totally different life and character, and the nation is interested in preserving both types, on both physical and moral grounds. The average physique of the factory operative cannot be entirely ascribed to preventible hygienic conditions.

(6.) Lastly, there are those who think the object of legislation should be to secure a maximum *net* surplus from the soil, which, it will be easily seen, does not necessarily follow from a maximum gross produce, and, indeed, in many respects these depend upon opposing causes: *e.g.*, the *gross* produce might be greatest under a system of small farms, and the *net* under the large system. Still, as Mill points out, this is by no means necessarily the case. It is true that under the small system of cultivation the non-agricultural population will bear a less *ratio* to the agricultural, but that it will be less numerous absolutely is by no means a consequence. The greater productiveness of the small cultivators may enable them both to consume a larger quantity of food themselves in the country, and yet to send a larger quantity to the towns. But although Mill's exception is theoretically sound, it can hardly be doubted that in practice—especially with the scientific agriculture of Great Britain—the net surplus would be greater under the large system. The advantage of a large net surplus is obvious if the country is self-supporting, for it determines the proportion of the population who can be employed in trades and professions non-agricultural, and if the country is not self-supporting, it is clear that it will gain the more it becomes so in the natural order of progress. A country with a population mainly agricultural is always in danger of not having a sufficient net surplus to purchase the conveniences and luxuries of the towns, and is further liable to agrarian pauperism.

But *net surplus*, which is strictly the amount of agricultural produce not consumed by those who cultivate the land, is not to be confounded, as is often done, with rent. If agricultural wages and profits are high, a large part of the net surplus is at the disposal of the labourers and farmers.

But it is sometimes argued that land is most advantageously employed when it is let at the highest *rent*, and any action of Government aiming at some other use of the land is resented. The position is generally supported by the "right to do as one likes with one's own" argument already examined; but it finds a stronger foundation in the analogy to the profit obtained on other forms of capital. There can be no doubt that, under a system of free competition, in every branch of industry and commerce, profit, or the expectation of profit, determines the direction in which labour and capital shall be applied. It is true that the leadership of profit is not always to be applauded, even from an economic point of view; Adam Smith ascribed many evils to the high rate of profit obtained in the colonial trade, and he always carefully distinguished between the profit to the capitalist and the advantage to the community of any trade or industry; and no one can maintain that the profit made by the exportation of adulterated goods is likely to be advantageous in the long-run, or that the profit which leads to the degradation of labour is not even more injurious ultimately. But, except where under the occasional pressure of social and moral considerations an exception is made, profit is allowed to control the employment of capital, and on analogy it may be fairly argued maximum rent should control the employment of land—unless some exceptional injury is found to ensue.

It cannot, I think, be denied that in every one of these objects to which the attention of Government is directed there is an element of goodness. It is expedient to preserve the sentiment that at present attaches itself to private property; it is desirable that the mass of the people should be more interested in the ownership of land; an increase in the gross produce of the soil would, *ceteris paribus*, be a national benefit; to let land at its highest rent, as a rule, secures its most advantageous use; and to be independent of foreign countries for the national food supply, and to possess a contented and numerous rural population, are both objects of great political and social importance. It is the object of the present work to investigate how far these various principles admit of reconciliation in some important problems connected with land, for there can be no doubt that if any legislation, positive or negative, can be suggested where the interests of the parties are in the main identical, such legislation should be accomplished without delay. In some cases where there is an apparent conflict between landlord and tenant, I have attempted to indicate the way the casting vote of the public should be given; but the precise weight to be attached to conflicting principles can only be determined after long political agitation, and the main object of the present work is rather to call attention to the convergence than to the divergence of interests.

CHAPTER III.

ON THE ECONOMIC RESULTS OF A SIMPLE SYSTEM OF TRANSFER OF PROPERTY IN LAND.

"The oak scorns to grow except on Free Land."

Old Proverb.[1]

THE difficulties which beset the transfer of landed property in this country have been so often and so graphically described by both lawyers and laymen that any detailed account of them in the present work would be quite superfluous. No one can doubt that the greater part of these difficulties are artificial and unnecessary; they are survivals of a different order of things; they can only be understood by a reference to the remote past. "The codification of the law of real property is not worth seeking for. Its principles and practice are so abstract that no code would render them intelligible to the public."[2] "Even now a purchase deed of a piece of freehold land cannot be explained without going back to the

[1] Quoted in Joshua Williams's *Real Property*, p. 369.

[2] Smith's *Mercantile Law*; Introduction, p. 14.

reign of Henry VIII., or an ordinary settlement of land without recourse to the laws of Edward I."[1]

But laws which have no other *raison d'être* than their antiquity cannot be maintained in an age when every institution is being put upon its trial; and every year witnesses a further abandonment of mediæval customs, and a nearer approach to rationality. Whether these gradual changes are more properly described as tinkering or as development is a question for lawyers and statesmen, but of the ultimate result of the process no doubt can be entertained. There are only two classes in the community who are supposed to have any interest in the preservation of the existing system—the present owners of land and the lawyers, and it may be doubted whether, if a more natural system of transfer were adopted, the real interests of either class would suffer. As regards lawyers it may be urged that the simplicity and the rationality of the principles of mercantile law have not injured their business; and although the technical skill which conveyancers have laboriously acquired must become valueless, the legal profession on the whole will probably not suffer by the reforms which are inevitable. It must be acknowledged that many of the most important reforms in law have been instituted and carried through by lawyers; and that when they have opposed changes, they have

[1] Joshua Williams's *Real Property*, p. 17.

been actuated by traditionary respect for old principles and methods, and not by feelings of class interest. But in any case, mere professional opposition could be of no avail even if offered, for the interests of a particular class can no longer look for protection. From an economic point of view lawyers must be classed with soldiers and policemen as necessary evils in a civilised society; the less their services are required so much the better. It is not denied that the practice of law calls forth the highest ability, but so also does the practice of war and the practice of physic; and wars, diseases, and lawsuits must cause more waste and suffering to the community than good and profit to the professional classes interested.

As regards the present landowners, the other portion of the community who suppose their interests would be injuriously affected by any radical changes in the present system of the law, it is by no means easy to decide whether this might not to some extent be the case, and even whether in some respects the nation at large might not lose, although compensated by other and presumably greater advantages. The size of estates, the House of Lords, the number of interests in any estate, the political and social influence attached to the ownership of land, the custom of primogeniture and of keeping up old families, the cordial relations between landlord and tenant, the absence of rack-renting, the voluntary remissions of rent in times of depression, have all been ascribed to the laws affecting the ownership of land; and it must be acknowledged that there is an element of goodness in all these peculiar portions of our land system. Even the large estates which are so frequently condemned have their advantages—a lord is as a rule in all respects better than a laird. The British aristocracy is certainly superior in its economic and social functions to the aristocracies of continental nations, and probably superior to their peasant proprietors. The classes interested in the ownership of land in this country, and in these far more than the merely nominal owners must be included, have probably as much influence on national life as the peasantry of France and Germany; and while both classes are conservative, the former are more intelligent and imbued with sounder political traditions. The younger sons of landed families, far more than the sons of our merchant princes, have to undergo the ordeal of the struggle for existence, and they contribute more recruits to the honourable professions. Adam Smith's opinion on the relative worth and breadth of view of country gentlemen and of merchants is well known: "It was probably in imitation of them [the merchants],and to put themselves on a level with those who they found were disposed to oppress them, that the country gentlemen and farmers of Great Britain so far forgot the generosity that is natural to their station as to demand the exclusive privilege of supplying their countrymen with corn and butcher's meat."

Old landed families, protected as they are by entails, settlements, and primogeniture, yield in return certain advantages. The landlord feels in most cases the weight of a slowly-accumulated responsibility. He would no more think of acting unfairly by his land and tenants than of acting with cowardice in the field or with injustice on the bench. And the influence of traditional sentiment is often an important factor in the relations of landlord and tenant;—the old large proprietors in Ireland may in some cases have been bad, but the new commercial proprietors were immeasurably worse. Granted that all landlords are tyrants, a big tyrant is always better than a little one—the former must act on certain rules and traditions, whilst the latter need only consult his own caprice. The finest system of law the world has produced grew up under the Roman emperors, and the most cruel sufferings ever endured were under Roman provincial governors.

In many respects land in small quantities is not a good source of income. A small landowner generally finds his rental insufficient, and if he does not burden his estate with mortgages, he has no capital for permanent improvements; he cannot afford to have his land unlet; it is of importance to him to get the highest rent. Hence it is probable that the objections made in Scotland to the landlord's hypothec were principally founded on the conduct of the smaller owners. If one or two farms of a large landowner are not let, the rest operate in the way of insurance, and he is more ready to submit to a general reduction of rents when necessary. In the recent remissions of rent the largest were certainly on the large estates. It must be remembered that large estates do not necessarily imply large farms, as the Duke of Argyll has recently shown by statistics. The ownership of land has no necessary connection with the size of farms; the largest proprietors in Scotland let some of their land to crofters, and, on the other hand, large farmers often hold land under different owners.

But when every allowance has been made for the advantages of the present system of large estates, two questions are naturally suggested—(1) whether the advantages really depend on the present artificial and costly land laws? and (2) whether the advantages are worth the cost? The same considerations apply to the answers to both questions, and they may be discussed together.

(1.) The advantages enumerated depend on the assumption that the nominal owner is the real owner, or at least that his resources are not seriously crippled by burdens on the estate. A needy landowner is of all poor people the most needy;

he can neither perform his social functions nor his moral duties. He cannot reside on his estates; he cannot effect improvements. So far as the production from the soil is concerned, both gross and net produce would be increased if encumbered estates were thrown on the market. The fact is generally acknowledged, and requires no illustration.

(2.) The respect for private property in land would be strengthened in proportion as ownership became real instead of being nominal. The socialistic outcry against landlords is largely founded on the abuses of nominal ownership. The sentiment of this country is naturally individualistic; the denunciation of capital by continental socialists finds very feeble and scanty approval in Great Britain. A large employer of labour, whom German working men would accuse of plundering the people, may amass a fortune, and, without any appearance of inconsistency, make speeches on the unearned increments from land. A socialist who writes to catch the ear of the British workman must begin and end with the land.

The ideas on which the hostility to landlordism rests have been very well formulated by John Stuart Mill. A considerable rise in rent may take place without any effort whatever on the part of proprietors; the rents of even absentee landlords may continually rise with the progress of society. At present a tenant may be subjected to a rise in rent on his own improvements; in the case of land the unearned increment is very palpable. But it is probably the social and political influences which indirectly spring from the possession of land, and the fact that the great estates of many noble families can be traced back to the scandalous misappropriation of public land, to which the feeling of the injustice of private property in land is principally to be attributed. The power of a great landowner is extreme : *e.g.* as the law stands, he can depopulate whole districts ; he may evict on social, religious, or political grounds, and, especially in the case of crofter holdings, by means of factors and ground officers, exercise a petty tyranny in the smallest affairs of life ; and that such power should be due to descent merely is galling to those who have to rely on their own labour. If the land with its inherent rights had not been kept in certain families by a highly artificial system of law, it may be doubted if in this country the outcry against landlords would ever have been greater than against capitalists. The very persons who most strongly object to the rights of large landowners are loudest in support of the advantages of similar rights in smaller owners. M. de Laveleye tells us that the land of small owners in Flanders is always let at a rack-rent, and there is no sense of injustice. If, however, there were no artificial restraints on the transfer of land, and if the social and political advantages attached to the possession of land, so far as they spring from the law, were abolished, the people of this country would probably no more object to large estates than they do to the possession of fleets of ships or acres of factories, and the respect for private property would be considerably strengthened.

(3.) But however simple the system of transfer were made, if everything in the nature of settlements were abolished, if Parliamentary titles were given and registration made compulsory, it is doubtful if in Great Britain there would be any great extension of the number of small owners. No farmer would think of buying land if he could rent it on fair terms; he could not afford to obtain from a large part of his capital only two or three per cent. by landowning, when ten per cent. might be made by farming. Still less would the labourer, who had the industry and courage to save, think of investing in the home country when he could obtain a far better field for his labour and capital abroad. Every year the obstacles, whether sentimental or mechanical, to emigration become less and less; and it is just those men who might have become peasant proprietors who are most ready to emigrate. If any increase in the number of small estates might be expected, it would be from the purchase of residential estates by the wealthy mercantile classes, from which nothing but good alike to merchants and country gentlemen could be anticipated.

(4.) The tendency of the reforms indicated would

no doubt be to put the relations of landlord and tenant on a more commercial footing; but there is a general feeling that, apart from questions of ownership, these relations and the mutual rights of the parties must be more strictly defined, and that matters of compensation, tenure, and the like cannot be left to the forbearance or generosity of the landlord. If, however, the old restrictions on ownership are retained, there must be much greater interference with freedom of contract than would be necessary if they were abolished. Any restraint on commerce and industry implies further restraints; customs involve excise duties, and *vice versa*; if one article is taxed, all possible substitutes must be taxed; and in the same way law begets law; any law in favour of one class involves countervailing laws to put other classes on the same footing. Preferential laws in favour of the landlord must be met by laws in favour of the tenant, but the more the former are diminished the less need will there be for the latter. How far the transfer of land admits of simplification is a question for lawyers, but it may be useful to point out that land can never be so easily transferred as other forms of property (*e.g.* Consols). In the words of Mr. Osborne Morgan, "stock possesses no boundaries, conceals no minerals, supports no game, pays no tithes, admits of no easements, is let to no tenant, and is hampered with no adjoining owners."[1]

[1] *Land Law Reform in England*, p. 10.

CHAPTER IV.

THE LAW OF DIMINISHING RETURN TO LAND.

"This general law of agricultural industry is the most important proposition in political economy." MILL.

"THE laws and the conditions of the production of wealth partake of the character of physical truths. There is nothing optional or arbitrary in them. Whatever mankind produce must be produced in the modes and under the conditions imposed by the constitution of external things, and by the inherent properties of their own bodily and mental structure. . . . Whether they like it or not, a double quantity of labour will not raise on the same land a double quantity of food, unless some improvement takes place in the processes of cultivation. . . . It is not so with the distribution of wealth. That is a matter of human institution solely. The things once there, mankind individually or collectively can do with them as they like. They can place them at the disposal of whomsoever they please, and on whatever terms. . . . The distribution of wealth depends on the laws and customs of society."[1] Mill says in his *Autobiography*, that the distinction here drawn between the laws of the production and those of the distribution of wealth was, in his opinion, the most important contribution he made to Political Economy. Once pointed out, the distinction seems natural and obvious, and yet the abuse that is showered on the "current" Political Economy, and the vague appeals to the fundamental principles of that science, show that, if apprehended, the distinction is disregarded. But it is of the utmost importance to discover, in the first place, to which class any so-called economic law belongs. Large-hearted philanthropists may be fighting against the iron laws of nature, and not, as they suppose, against the earthen laws of men; and Socialism often clamours more loudly against the former than against the latter.

Most of the theories of Political Economy are complex—they partake of the character of the unalterable laws of nature as well as of the laws and customs of human institution,—and in all cases, where practical reforms are intended, the two elements must be carefully separated. Nowhere is this separation so necessary as in the theory of Population of Malthus, and the theory of Rent of Ricardo.

[1] Mill's *Principles of Political Economy*, bk. ii. ch. i. sect. 1.

In both theories there are certain necessary and certain voluntary elements, and the upholders of one extreme view reduce the voluntary to the necessary, whilst their opponents reduce the necessary to the voluntary. The former maintain, for example, that population must be always pressing on subsistence, and the latter, that there is no necessary limit to the increase of population; the former maintain there must always be paupers, the latter, that there is always a sufficiency of food, and abundance of work; the former ascribe poverty to the niggardliness of nature, the latter to the injustice of man.

The best illustration of those laws of the production of wealth "which partake of the character of physical truths" is found in the law of diminishing return. The law lies at the basis of the Malthusian theory of Population, and of the Ricardian theory of Rent. It can be expressed in one of those propositions, so common in political economy, which seem necessarily true as soon as stated, and yet which, when applied for practical purposes, are very likely through this very simplicity to give rise to errors.

The law may be thus stated in its strictest form: "If to any given piece of land [other things remaining the same] labour and capital [of the same efficiency per unit] be applied continuously, beyond a certain point the return per unit will diminish." The qualifying clauses, in brackets, demand particular attention, because the errors which arise in the application of the law are mainly due to the omission of these necessary conditions of its validity. It might happen, for instance, that the piece of land taken is improved by arterial drainage, or by other operations on neighbouring land; and obviously, any improvement in the arts of production, which is the same thing as an increase in the efficiency of the capital and labour, will counteract the law for the time. Again, it should be observed that the diminishing return per unit of labour and capital will, beyond a certain point, become *nil*, and eventually a negative quantity, or positively injurious to the land. A simple example of this is presented by the case of artificial manure; up to a certain point every additional unit (*e.g.* of ammonia) will give an equal or even increasing return, but at a later stage the returns will begin to diminish, and at a still later stage further application may be positively injurious.

From the general law an important deduction can at once be made. A farmer, farming for profit, will endeavour to apply capital just up to the point at which, after paying landlord's rent, he obtains the ordinary rate of farming profits, or at any rate no further than he can afford to pay the ordinary rate of wages; but a peasant proprietor, who regards the whole crop as a return to labour, will be apt to extend his labour till the return reaches the vanishing-point; accordingly, if the methods of production are in both cases the same, the gross return will be greater in the latter case than in the former. But even the industry of the peasant proprietor must, at some point, find its limit, and all the labour after a certain point, although increasing the gross produce, must *pro tanto* be considered a national loss. The farmer ceases to employ labour when the additional return will not yield the wages of labour (including his own superintendence and trouble), but the peasant will work far beyond this point, and it is clear that, beyond this point, his labour would have been more advantageously employed in some other industry. Since, however, a small agriculturist cannot, as a rule, devote part of his time to his land, and part to other employment, it follows that, if the natural energies are to be employed to the best advantage, the size of the small holdings should be such as to prevent this waste of labour. No large farmer, *e.g.*, could afford to pay men or even women to creel sea-ware up steep cliffs to manure his land;—altogether apart from profit, he could not give the current rate of wages.

But any improvement in the methods of agriculture makes the advantageous application of additional labour and capital possible, so that the point of diminishing return is year after year pushed further. Land in this country produces, says Professor Thorold Rogers, probably seven times as much as it did five hundred years ago, and the increased production is due in the last resort to the increase of intelligence in the methods of production. It must also be observed that an improvement in the means of communication is equivalent to a direct improvement of the art of cultivation, for not only does the farmer obtain his materials cheaper, but he loses less on the cost of carriage of his produce to market. In fact, as Mill has elaborately shown, there is scarcely any advance in general civilisation which may not indirectly counteract the law of diminishing return. But the general environment and the arts of cultivation remaining the same, this law is always operative so far as any given piece of land is concerned. The law, however, simple as it is, has been misunderstood and misapplied. On the one side it has been ignored by the practical man—*e.g.* during the recent depression one of the most frequent assertions was that the only remedy consisted in the further application of capital to land. So far as this application was prevented by want of security, restrictions of landlords, excessive preservation of game, etc., the proposal was no doubt justified, and will be examined later on; but generally more than this was intended, and the opinion still widely obtains that there is practically no limit to the employment of capital in agriculture.

But on the other hand, it must be confessed that the application of the law of diminishing return, especially when coupled with the proposition that land is limited in quantity, generally errs in the opposite direction. People are too readily inclined to suppose a country, or tract of country, calls for a diminution rather than an increase of the capital and labour devoted to agriculture. They are inclined to lay too much stress on the possible waste of labour and capital in small holdings; they forget that produce may fall short of its maximum owing to a dearth of capital and labour.

Again, theoretical writers, and Mill is the chief offender, too often suppose, in spite of their own previous qualifications, that what is true "ultimately" is true always. They argue, for instance, that in old countries cultivation is always carried to the point of diminishing return, and they forget that so long as a law is counteracted, the counteracting cause is the more important matter to be considered. For example, in considering the increase of population, too much stress is laid on the law under examination and too little on the exceptions. I do not say the exceptions are not mentioned, but that the force of attention is misdirected. This will find better illustration in the next chapter.

It only remains to point out that the law of diminishing return gives rise to the most important differences between agricultural products and manufactures, both as regards quantity and value. No doubt even in manufactures the law in its strictest sense is operative. Within the walls of a certain factory, and with a certain amount of machinery, the application of labour and capital is limited, but so far as any country is concerned, the extension of the instruments of manufactures is practically unlimited, whilst the instrument land cannot be increased. Manufactures can be increased by both the intensive and extensive application of capital; agriculture after a certain point only by its intensive application. It would be easy to multiply manifold the amount of manufactures at the same or even at a diminishing cost, if the requisite labour and capital were forthcoming, although the production of food had already reached its limit.[1] It follows then that Mill was in error in supposing that the limited quantity and limited productiveness of land are the real limits to the increase of production. They constitute, no doubt, the limits to the production of agricultural wealth, but not of wealth in general; and it follows, too, that any artificial attempt to foster agriculture at the expense of manufactures would, if it succeeded, cause a national economic loss.

[1] Compare the enormous increase in the production of manufactures since the introduction of machinery about the end of last century.

CHAPTER V.

MALTHUS AND THE CROFTERS.

"That an increase in the population, when it follows in its natural order, is both a great positive good in itself and absolutely necessary to a further increase in the annual produce of the land and labour of any country, I should be the last to deny."—MALTHUS, *Essay on Population.*

PROBABLY no writer of repute ever incurred such universal and undeserved odium as the Rev. T. R. Malthus, sometime Professor of Political Economy in the East India College, Hertfordshire. Even now he is regarded as the author of a system or a prophecy that makes the outlook for humanity not merely dismal, but revolting. "Malthusianism," as popularly understood, "avowedly makes vice and suffering the necessary results of a natural instinct, with which are united the purest and sweetest affections;"[1] it ascribes all evils to the inevitable pressure of population on subsistence; it cries aloud, "The only salvation for mankind lies in checks to population; emigration may retard, but it cannot for long postpone, the inevitable fate,—the time must come when

[1] *Progress and Poverty*, p. 85.

famine and disease can alone relieve the pressure on the soil." A plain statement then of what Malthus actually wrote, and the bearing of his doctrines on certain aspects of the present land agitation, seems desirable.

Like most writers of the first rank, Malthus was very much influenced by the circumstances of the age in which he wrote. In the first place, Godwin, Condorcet, and others were dazzling the working classes with visionary systems of equality; and secondly, the country had adopted a system of poor laws which not only degraded labour but threatened the whole country with ruin. The central idea of the system appeared to be to encourage population; wages were supplemented from the rates according to the number of children, and even illegitimate children, or rather their mothers, were treated by the law with the greatest tenderness. It had been remarked that the most populous nations were the most prosperous, and it was supposed that the increase of population must involve the increase of prosperity. Even Adam Smith said that the most decisive mark of the prosperity of any country is the increase of the number of its inhabitants. The poor man was told that to raise up subjects for his king and country was a most meritorious act, and statesmen were in continual dread of a falling-off in the recruits for their fleets and armies. Uncultivated land was looked at askance, and commons were enclosed to increase the supply of food and the number of people, whilst emigration was strictly prohibited. At the same time, the country was practically dependent on its own food supplies; the minimum price for the free importation of corn was continually being raised.

Speaking generally, it may be affirmed that the economic conditions under which Malthus wrote were exactly the opposite of those generally prevailing at the present time in this country. The present system of poor relief is no doubt capable of much improvement, but it at least recognises the fundamental principle that relief must be not merely remedial but preventive. Again, not only are there greater facilities for emigration, owing to the improved means of communication and more accurate knowledge, but many of our colonies encourage immigration by bounties in the shape of free passage; and lastly, we can purchase as much food as we require with our manufactures—the new world is rapidly becoming the granary of the old. Accordingly the fundamental doctrine of Malthus can no longer be presented with the local colouring which made it so striking on its first appearance; the area of Great Britain to which it applies is comparatively small, and the time when it will again excite public attention comparatively distant. And yet on several grounds the theory requires attention and examination at the present time. Just as the doctrine of

Malthus was at first the natural reaction against the doctrine of equality, so now the doctrine of equality is appearing as the natural reaction to the theory of population; and in the moral and social sciences ideas tend to become realities; whilst the physical observer is only a spectator, the moral philosopher is an actor. If the expropriation of the landlords appear "good" to the sovereign people, whether it be good or not in reality, nothing can prevent the expropriation; popular government necessarily involves the realisation of popular ideas. Apart, too, from this general consideration, there are portions of the British Isles, not to mention India, where striking examples are presented of the Malthusian theory. Again, the rate of increase of population in America and the Colonies is such that in a few generations the field for emigration will be greatly narrowed; and if the present rate of increase in this country is maintained, over-population threatens to become a serious matter of consideration for the nation at large. Last year, taking the whole United Kingdom, loss by emigration amounted to about half the excess of births over deaths, in other words, half the natural increase was absorbed by other countries.

Malthus commences his Essay on Population by saying that it would be beyond the power of any individual to enumerate all the causes that have influenced human improvement, and that the principal object of his work is to examine the effects of "one great cause intimately united with the very nature of man," that cause being "the constant tendency in all animated life to increase beyond the nourishment prepared for it." Thus at the very outset he guards himself from the imputation, which he has so frequently incurred, of ascribing all the ills of life to the one cause he has investigated. The theory, stated in his own words, is expressed in three propositions :—

"1. Population is necessarily limited by the means of subsistence.

2. Population invariably increases when the means of subsistence increases, unless prevented by some powerful and obvious checks.

3. These checks, and the checks which repress the superior power of population, and keep its effects on a level with the means of subsistence, are all resolvable into moral restraint, vice, and misery."

The first of these propositions is obviously true, but its importance can only be perceived when taken in connection with the law of diminishing return examined in the last chapter. The obvious deduction is, that population can increase faster than the means of subsistence, or, stated more definitely, that in any society more children may be born than can be reared to a healthy maturity by the means of subsistence at the command of the society.

The second proposition is given with an important qualification: "It should be observed that by an increase in the means of subsistence is here meant such an increase as will enable the mass of society to command more food. An increase might certainly take place which, in the actual state of a particular society, would not be distributed to the lower classes, and, consequently, would give no stimulus to population." In this statement Malthus follows Adam Smith: "Every species of animals naturally multiplies in proportion to the means of their subsistence, and no species can ever multiply beyond it. But in civilised society it is only among the inferior ranks of people that the scantiness of subsistence can set limits to the further multiplication of the human species."[1] It is quite possible then that the population of any country may be much lower than its resources would beneficially admit of, and may even decline simply on account of the unequal and unjust distribution of its wealth. But the advance on Adam Smith made by Malthus is contained in the third proposition. The former had written that the scantiness of subsistence could only operate by destroying a great part of the children which the fruitful marriages (of the common people) produce; but the latter only brings in this and other positive checks as an alternative to the checks classed as preventive. Of both classes Malthus makes an elaborate examination,

[1] *Wealth of Nations*, bk. i. ch. viii.

taking a survey of nearly all the countries in the world. But he has paid the usual penalty for attempting to be judicial on a subject where the current of prejudices runs strong. He has been supposed by some to maintain that over-population was inevitable, and that the poor should be left to starve; by others he is regarded as approving of any means whatever of preventing the increase of population, of laws directly forbidding marriage, of infanticide, and of abortion. No charges were ever more devoid of foundation. His object was to persuade men to use the reason which distinguishes them from all other creatures to prevent the destruction and degradation of life which prevails throughout the rest of the animal world. He endeavoured to impress upon public opinion that "it is not the duty of man simply to propagate his species, but to propagate virtue and happiness, and that if he has not a tolerably fair prospect of doing this he is by no means called upon to leave descendants." He struck straight at the notion universally prevalent at the end of last century, that population should be encouraged in every way, and insisted that quality as well as numbers should be regarded. It is true that he advocated the very gradual abolition of the poor-laws, but simply on the ground which was perfectly valid when he wrote, that they had deteriorated and not ameliorated the condition of the mass of the people. But he proposed remedies, the very opposite of those usually connected with his name. He writes: "In most countries, among the lower classes of people, there appears to be something like a standard of wretchedness, a point below which they will not continue to marry and propagate their species. This standard is different in different countries, and is formed by various concurring circumstances of soil, climate, government, degree of knowledge, civilisation, etc. The principal circumstances which contribute to raise it, are liberty, security of property, the diffusion of knowledge, and a taste for the conveniences and comforts of life. Those which contribute principally to lower it are despotism and ignorance. In an attempt to better the condition of the labouring classes of society, our object should be to raise this standard as high as possible by cultivating a spirit of independence, a decent pride, and a taste for cleanliness and comfort. . . . The fairest chance of accomplishing this end would probably be by the establishment of a system of parochial education upon a plan similar to that proposed by Adam Smith."

Whether a country is over-populated or not cannot be determined by a few simple sums in addition and division. It is futile to divide the aggregate wealth by the number of people, still more futile to take as dividend the aggregate amount of wealth possible under some ideal scheme. The positive laws of a country permit a certain distribution of wealth, and the system of production has these laws for its basis. Positive law admits of gradual reform, but in the meantime the remedies proposed for any evil must have regard to that law as one of the factors to be taken into account. So long as private property in land is permitted, the fact must be considered in any attempt to increase the numbers or quality of the rural population. We cannot, accordingly, simply determine the natural resources of a district, and its capability of supporting a larger population, and then advocate changes in the law founded on a special case. We must consider, in the first place, whether the increase of numbers is desirable; and, secondly, whether the desirability is sufficiently great to require the intervention of Government, and radical changes in the conception of private property.

There can be no doubt that the population of the Highlands is as great as the standard of comfort of the people and their command over wealth admit of under the present positive law; it may even be asserted that their standard of comfort is in many places low, and, considering the resources at their disposal, the population excessive. So far as the present generation is concerned, it may be granted that the position of the crofters would immediately be much improved by an extension of their crofts, and by allowing them additional grazings. It is probable that for some time they might be able and willing to pay the rents; they might even pay more than large farmers for the particular portions of land they occupied. But all this would, according to the teaching of Malthus, in a few years be of no avail, unless the condition of the crofters, morally and intellectually, were raised at the same time, and unless they clearly recognised themselves that any subdivision of their lots (or rights to hill pasture) would be fatal to their prosperity; or unless, as an alternative, they were content to submit to regulations such as are so beneficially enforced in Sutherland. So long as the standard of wretchedness is as low as it seems at present to be in Skye, Lewis, and other islands on the west coast, an extension of crofter holdings without guarantees against subdivision could only result in the extension of the area of agrarian pauperism. Relief not to be injurious must be preventive as well as remedial. Merely to enlarge the present holdings would soon be equivalent in its effects to the increase in wages by the parochial authorities under the old poor-law; if nothing else were done the advantages could be only temporary, for population would increase down to the former standard. Only those who still retain the eighteenth century notions of the necessity of supplying fleets and armies, and of replenishing the earth with people, can find pleasure in such a prospect.

The position of the crofters bears a strong resemblance to the position of the working-classes in England at the end of last century and the commencement of this, when the small gave way to the large system of industry. In the first half of the eighteenth century the large system of industry was practically unknown; workmen were engaged by the year, they were obliged to serve an apprenticeship, which restrained undue competition, and the magistrates were, according to the Act (5th Elizabeth), "to assess the wages, so as to yield unto the hired person, both in the time of scarcity and the time of plenty, a convenient proportion of wages." Under the old conditions this law and its corresponding customs seem in general to have worked to the satisfaction of both masters and men. But with the introduction of machinery and the factory system, the old customs were necessarily abandoned. During the period of transition the labourers suffered severely, but after they became accustomed to the new order of things, and recognised their position, their condition gradually improved, and still continues to improve. At first they were content with petitions to Parliament to enforce the old customs—they deemed Parliament omnipotent. The evils for which they sought redress were incomparably greater than those complained of by the Highland crofters. Consider the case of the framework knitters of Nottingham,[1] when they petitioned Parliament on

[1] Brentano, *Origin of Guilds and Trade Unions*, p. 119.

the 2d of February 1779. "After various deductions which the workmen had to submit to—for frame-rent, winding, seaming, needles, candles, etc., their wages are stated as 6s. or 8s. weekly. . . . The value of a frame is stated as £6 or £8. But for its use the workmen had to pay rents from 1s. 3d. to 2s. a week; that is, up to 86 per cent. The workmen were obliged to hire these frames, if they wished to get work; if a workman had himself a frame, he was refused work," etc. etc. Throughout the whole range of industry the condition of the working-classes was not much better, and in some cases, *e.g.* in that of the calico printers, it was worse. These evils have been remedied partly by the factory legislation, but, for the most part, the improvement has been due to the free play of economic laws. There was no attempt to fix the rate of wages or the term of employment; there was no attempt to protect declining industries; in spite of the introduction of power-looms, the number of hand-loom weavers for a time actually increased, but they were left to reap the reward of their own infatuation. Government, it is true, attempted to provide judicial arbitrators in some cases[1] of dispute between masters and men (*e.g.* in the cotton industry), but the attempts were abortive.

Still in many other ways Government found it necessary to interfere, and the list of sanitary and

[1] *Cf.* Statutes, 40 Geo. III. c. 90; 43 Geo. III. c. 151; 44 Geo. III. c. 87.

other conditions under which alone labour can be employed has been steadily extended since the first introduction of factory legislation; and it may be asserted without fear of contradiction, that in nearly every important industry the Government has interfered, not to control the contracts made between masters and men, as to the rate of wages, but to regulate the conditions under which alone any capitalist may employ hired labour. "We have to-day a complete, minute, and voluminous code for the protection of labour; buildings must be kept pure of effluvia; dangerous machinery must be fenced; children and young persons must not clean it while in motion; their hours are not only limited, but fixed; continuous employment must not exceed a given number of hours, varying with the trade, but prescribed by law in given cases; a statutable number of holidays is imposed; the children must go to school, and the employer must every week have a certificate to that effect; if an accident happens, notice must be sent to the proper authorities; special provisions are made for bake-houses, for lace-making, for collieries, and for a whole schedule of other special callings; for the due enforcement and vigilant supervision of this immense host of minute prescriptions there is an immense host of inspectors, certifying surgeons, and other authorities, whose business it is 'to speed and post o'er land and ocean,' in restless guardianship of every kind of labour, from that of the woman who plaits straw at her cottage door to the miner who descends into the bowels of the earth, and the seaman who conveys the fruits and materials of universal industry to and fro between the remotest parts of the globe."[1]

The question naturally arises, Has not the principle which underlies this multiform interference a legitimate application to the case of small agricultural holdings? In what respect do these small holders essentially differ from the labourers in other industries? Must they not also work under certain conditions? May they not also, if left to freedom of contract, submit to terms injurious to their moral and physical well-being? Can they trust simply to the wisdom and philanthropy of the landowners? The evil under which this class of the community labours is obvious, and its causes are obvious. There can be no doubt that the small size of the holdings is the main feature of the distress, and this minute subdivision must be due either to the action of the landlords, who have had to provide for the families removed from other places, or to the imprudent increase of the home-staying population, due to the small tenants themselves. There can be no doubt that the latter is by far the most important cause of the evil. In the most remote parts of Sutherland, where subdivision is strictly prevented by the proprietor, the peasantry can, for comfort, be

[1] Morley's *Life of Cobden*, vol. i. p. 303.

favourably compared with any peasantry in Europe. But such regulations cannot always be enforced by a proprietor, even if he wishes to do so;—"Man is, of all baggage, the most difficult to be transported;" and (as in Ireland) the letter of the regulations may be kept whilst the spirit is evaded. But, if ever the population of the Highlands and Islands of Scotland is to be prosperous, in some way or other, either by the voluntary action of the people, or by the strict control of the landlord, or, finally, by the direct intervention of Government, subdivision of lots or undue increase of population in the area let in small holdings must be prevented. The first method has confessedly failed, the second is only partially adopted, so that the adoption of the third appears inevitable. Government fixes the number of cubic inches of air necessary for factories and schools; it regulates the number of passengers and the amount of cargo a vessel may carry; it compels the owners of houses to make them habitable; and on analogy, there seems no obvious reason, either theoretical or practical, why the Legislature should not make it absolutely illegal for land to be let to more people than it can support, account of course being taken of the subsidiary industries (*e.g.* fishing), of which the population habitually avail themselves. There would thus be a national gain so far as the production of wealth is concerned, and without doubt there would, in a short time, be a still greater gain through the elevation of the standard of wretchedness of the people. Emigration would be, as in Sutherland, only indirectly compulsory, but the greatest incentive would be given to the members of the family who were not to succeed to the holding to look for employment elsewhere. The interference with the rights of property would really be very slight, and can be justified by the strongest analogy. No farmer is allowed to put more stock on a grass park than it will carry; to starve sheep or cattle is an offence against the law; and if a landed proprietor wishes to have any portion of his land let to crofters, let him be compelled to let it to them in sufficiently large portions to ensure them subsistence. There can be no doubt that the landlord would gain if such a law were enforced; minute subdivision leads in the first place to arrears, and eventually to an increase of the poor rates; whilst with larger holdings the crofters could adopt a better system of cultivation (especially if they formed club farms), and could afford to pay, and pay with regularity, a much higher rent. Whether a proprietor is morally bound or should be legally compelled to let some portion of his estates to crofters is a far more difficult problem, and can be more conveniently discussed in a later chapter. (Ch. XI.)

CHAPTER VI.

RICARDO'S THEORY OF RENT.

"Si Ricardo revenait dans ce monde, pourrait-il en présence de tous ces maux qui frappent l'agriculture des vieilles sociétés soutenir que le propriétaire foncier est un être privilégié, le favori de la civilisation, qui voit ses bénéfices croître sans cesse, sans travail, et qui prélève la meilleure part sur les produits des progrès sociaux?"
Essai sur la Répartition des Richesses.

P. LEROY-BEAULIEU.

THE theory of rent generally adopted by English economists is called after the name of Ricardo, not because he was the first to propound the theory, but because he drew certain extremely paradoxical conclusions from it which startled the public,—for example, that improvements always in the first place tend to lower rent; that if all rents were abolished, there would be no effect on the price of agricultural produce; and that in the progress of society rents must continuously rise (apart from improvements), owing to the pressure of population on the means of subsistence, and the consequent necessity of resorting to inferior land, or of cultivating the old land more highly. Ricardo was an admirable logician, and if we can only find out the assumptions he makes in his arguments, his conclusions are almost always correct. But his style is as unadorned as that of Euclid, and his mode of presenting a subject is the same as if Euclid had omitted altogether the definitions, axioms, and postulates, and drawn the propositions at random from a ballot-box. It will then be better to substitute the exposition of the theory of rent by some later writer for the "original Greek" of Ricardo.

The following passage from the late Professor Cairnes seems well adapted to give a preliminary idea of the theory: "In the first place, what are the assumptions on which the theory of rent is founded? It assumes first that of the whole agricultural produce of the country, those portions which in the market are sold at the same price are not all raised at the same cost; and, secondly, the price at which the whole crop sells is regulated by the cost of producing that portion of it which is produced at greatest expense. If these two points be granted, the existence of a surplus value, or, as we may call it, 'economic rent,' is a logical necessity which it is impossible to evade; and if we take further into account the motives which actuate farmers in hiring and landlords in letting land, we shall see that it is equally a logical necessity that, under the action of competition, this 'economic rent' should pass to the proprietor of the soil."[1] If the crop raised at the greatest expense was not sold at a price sufficient to replace the capital with profits, that land on which it was raised would go out of cultivation, and then the diminution of supply would tend to raise the price until it was again profitable to cultivate this "land on the margin of cultivation," as it is termed. For it is supposed, owing to the law of diminishing return, that the *additional* supply could only be obtained from the more fertile land at a cost equal to that on the worst land in cultivation which pays no rent.

"Economic rent" arises from three principal causes, the operation of two of which is quite apparent, whilst the working of the third is not altogether so simple and obvious. The first two causes are fertility, and proximity to the market. Natural fertility may not admit of exact definition, but it cannot be doubted that if the same labour and capital have been devoted to different qualities of land for a considerable period, there will still be, owing to natural qualities, a difference in the yield. It is well known that in any district the relative values of different holdings, and of different fields on the same holding, often do not change for generations. The effect on rent of situation is too obvious to require explanation, the value of situation being reckoned by cost of carriage, climatic conditions, etc.

[1] *Logical Method of Political Economy*, p. 190.

The effect of the third cause is less evident. Suppose that all the land of a country is equally fertile, and the situation of every holding in relation to the market and to the climate equally favourable—Will the land pay rent, and if so, why? If at any time the price of agricultural produce is just sufficient to return the farmer capital and the ordinary rate of profit, it is clear there can be no surplus for rent; but suppose that owing to the increase of population the demand for food increases and its price rises. In this case the farmers will apply more capital and labour to the land, and under the stimulus of the higher prices raise an additional supply. But owing to the law of diminishing return the additional supply can only be raised at an increasing cost, and if it is to be raised annually the price must remain high. It is argued, then, that if the extra capital applied yields the ordinary rate of profit at the new price, the old capital must yield more (for it yielded the ordinary rate at a lower price of produce), and this surplus constitutes economic rent. There can be no doubt that if, as is supposed, the cultivator ceases to apply capital just at the point where the return to an additional unit would be below the average rate of profit, in that case the units previously applied yield more than the ordinary rate, and the surplus goes to the landlord in the form of rent. But the point to which I think sufficient attention has not been directed is this—Why should the cultivator stop at this stage? Why does he not apply more capital still? for so long as the surplus in the previous applications is sufficient to make up the deficiency on the later, he will on the capital invested obtain the ordinary rate of profit. The usual answer is that if the cultivator is also owner it will pay him better to invest the additional capital in some other occupation that will yield the ordinary rate; for in that manner on the whole of his capital he obtains the usual rate of profit and on part of it a surplus profit in the shape of economic rent; if, on the other hand, the landlord and cultivator are different persons, the former will take care that just so much capital is applied to the land as to make net surplus a maximum.

The reasoning appears to be quite correct and the theory sound, but before applying a theory to practice it is necessary to take into account the assumptions on which it rests. It will be seen that the argument when the owner is also cultivator proceeds on the assumption that the owner can invest or employ his capital in some other occupation at the ordinary rate of profit. But practically, it must be observed, the cultivating landowner would not be able to invest his capital in anything but agriculture, so as to get the ordinary rate of *profit;* all he could expect on other investments is the ordinary rate of *interest.* Accordingly we find in practice that it might be advantageous for the cultivating *owner* to go beyond the point indicated. An illustration will make this clear. Let farming profits be 10 per cent., and the rate at which any surplus capital could be invested 4 per cent. In this case it would be better to employ all the capital on the land at 10 per cent., than half at 12 per cent. on the land and half at 4 per cent. in investments. In the former case the return on £10,000 would be £1000, and in the latter only £800. But suppose now that the owner lets the land. If the farmer is allowed to employ only £5000 of capital, and the return is 12 per cent., he will be able to pay £100 rent, since he only expects 10 per cent. on his capital, whereas if he employed the additional £5000, and secured just the ordinary rate of profit on the whole, viz. 10 per cent., he would be able to pay no rent. It follows, then, that according to the Ricardian theory of rent the landlord must place a check on the application of the farmer's capital if the latter is to receive the ordinary rate of profit and the former a maximum rent. To the landlord the amount of the gross produce is a matter of indifference, except so far as it bears on the net surplus; when once the point of maximum rent is determined, any further application of capital is resisted; but the tenant is interested in the gross produce and not in the net surplus; so long as he obtains the average rate of farming profits it is perfectly indifferent to him whether his rent is large or small.

The case just examined shows that the assertion

so confidently made that the existence of rent can make no difference to the farmers, is certainly not sound in theory, and in some respects not in practice, and other reasons may be given to prove that for land to yield a maximum rent *may* be to the advantage neither of the farmer nor of the public. (*a*) The kind of produce is fixed in the interests of the landlord. Here it is easy to take an extreme case by way of illustration. If a landlord has ground equally adapted for deer and sheep, he will be governed by the amount of rent. But it is clear deer forests benefit only the landlord and the shooting tenant; the produce is not worth considering—it would not even pay for the labour of the gillies and keepers. Again, to take a less extreme case: Arable land per unit employs more capital and labour than grazing land, but the latter may afford a higher rent, although the public at large may not be benefited. (*b*) The landlord is supposed to divide the land in such a way as to obtain a maximum rent. If the demand for small farms is great, and a lower rate of profits accepted by small tenants, the tendency will so far be towards small farms; if, on the other hand, the large system is much more efficient, then large farms may be preferred. But whatever the causes affecting the rent offered, we may suppose, social considerations apart, that the extent of the farms will be governed by the supposed interest of the landlord alone; and in fact one of the most common reasons given against compensation for buildings erected by the tenant is that the landlord at a future period might wish to divide or consolidate his farms. But here, again, it is quite clear that the interests of the landlord and the other parties concerned are not necessarily harmonious; *latifundia perdidere Italiam.* Howfar agriculture and the rural population have prospered in any countryunder the guidance of maximum rent must always form a difficult practical problem; in Ireland Government interference was thought to be necessary, and of late a considerable agitation has taken place in Great Britain—but it is sufficient here to point out that the existence of a separate rent-receiving class may, under certain circumstances, check production and to some extent raise prices.

But, on the other hand, there is an obvious advantage to the farmer in being able to rent land instead of being obliged to purchase; it requires as much capital to buy twenty acres as it does to farm a hundred. The farmer, in fact, borrows the land just as a trader or manufacturer borrows capital, and the tendency of economic progress has certainly been to separate the owners of capital who simply receive interest from the employers of capital, who receive profit in "wages of management." In the case of land, however, this separation is not nearly so complete as in other forms of capital; the lender of the land claims a share in the superintendence, and is often influenced by other than commercial reasons, giving preferential rents to more favoured tenants. The general tendency is, however, every day operating more and more in agriculture; restrictive clauses in leases are disappearing, and the farmer only requires security for his capital to assume the complete direction. The necessity for the change is due to the progressive character of agriculture at present; and the small success which seems to attend landowners farming their own land seems to show that the change will be proportionately more beneficial to them than to the tenants, for competition will always keep down farmers' profits to the ordinary rate, and rent is simply surplus profit.

To resume: Ricardo's theory may be taken as giving in the main a correct explanation of the reasons why at any particular time rent for land is paid at all, and why the rent is different in different cases; but the theory assumes that the amount of capital applied to land, the kind of produce, and the size of the holdings, are all determined by the landlord with the view of securing the maximum *net* produce. Accordingly the interests of the landlord, the tenant, and the public are not necessarily harmonious, but on other grounds the separation of the land-owning from the land-cultivating class seems on the whole favourable to the tenant and indirectly to the public through the increase in agricultural produce.

Hitherto we have regarded rent in the usual way as the payment made for the use of the farm and all the fixed capital which the landlord provides, but in the deductions from the theory of rent which give plausibility to schemes for the nationalisation of land, and the seizure by the State of "unearned increments," economic rent must be taken more strictly. It is supposed that the total landlord's rent can be divided into two parts—*first*, that part which is due to the labour of himself or his predecessors in title, and which may be called profit-rent; and, *secondly*, the remainder, which is due to causes over which the landlord has no control, *e.g.* improvement in the means of communication, increase of population causing increased demand for food, and, in fact, the general progress of society. It is only this second part which is supposed to be strictly economic rent, and it is ascribed to the original and indestructible powers of the soil, situation, and the like. Theoretically this distinction between profit-rent and economic-rent seems plausible, but some writers have thought the distinction cannot be maintained in practice. No doubt it is impossible to say, of any piece of land, how much of the fertility is natural and how much acquired, and to enumerate its original and indestructible powers; but all that is required is to compare one piece of land with other land in the district; for in all probability all land in the same neighbourhood has had in the course of ages about the same amount of labour and capital expended upon it, and accordingly any difference in the present rent points to a difference in the inherent qualities. Differences in situation seem to furnish a still better example of economic rent. It would be quite easy to calculate how much of the rent of a piece of land was due to its situation alone as distinct from its natural and acquired qualities.

We have seen that at any particular time (the arts of production remaining stationary and the country being supplied with food from its own resources alone) Ricardo's theory would explain the fact of rent and the differences in rent. But where the theory fails is in giving the reasons why "economic" rent has risen in the past, and why it may be expected to rise continuously in the future; and just as the socialistic agitation against private ownership of capital in general may be largely traced to Ricardo's doctrine of wages (the "natural" rate of wages being just the amount on which the labourers would consent to live and keep up their numbers), so the agitation against private ownership in land may be traced to the same writer's hypothetical history of the past, and prophecies on the future, of "economic rent."

The cause of the continuous rise in rent, according to Ricardo and his followers, is the constant pressure of population on the means of subsistence which makes it necessary either to resort to inferior land or to wring from the land already in cultivation the additional food required at an ever-increasing cost. In this manner the margin of cultivation is continually being pushed further and further, and the rent of the better lands is continually raised. No wonder there is a cry raised for unearned increments! Malthus is supposed to prove that population *must* increase faster than the means of subsistence from the soil under cultivation with the methods adopted at any time, and then Ricardo is quoted to prove that this increase must increase the cost of raising food, that poor land must submit to the plough, that good land must be strained to a greater intensity of cultivation, and that every increase in the difficulty of procuring food must *ipso facto* cause a corresponding rise in rent.

There is no doubt an element of truth in this as in most doctrines that have attained celebrity, and occasional examples are furnished by history of the process described. If a population is wholly or mainly engaged in rural pursuits, we may find the increase in numbers directly stimulating cultivation and raising rents. But as a rule, as Professor Thorold Rogers has pointed out, and no one has a better claim to authority on the history of agriculture, "the development of agriculture, the advantageous cultivation of inferior soils, goes on simultaneously with the numerical decline of that part of the population which labours on and is directly subsisted by the soil." In fact, an undue increase of rural population, involving, as it generally does, minute subdivision of the soil, is likely to make landlords' rents (both "profit" and "economic") disappear altogether rather than to increase them.

Where an increase of population tends to raise rents, it will generally be found to be an increase of the town and not of the rural population, in the manner described by Adam Smith in the chapter entitled, "How the Commerce of Towns contributed to the Improvement of the Country."[1] He asserts that the cultivation of the soil was extended and intensified, in order to obtain the luxuries of the towns; and in our own times the most plausible argument in favour of protection to new countries (*e.g.* Canada), is, that the development of towns is necessary for the development of agriculture.

But, after every allowance is made, the very reverse of the teaching of Ricardo in the progress of rent must be accepted as normally true. As Professor Thorold Rogers says: "It is not the pressure of population on the means of subsistence which has led men to cultivate inferior soils, but the fact that these soils being cultivated in another way, or taken into cultivation, an increased population became possible." A striking example is furnished by the enormous growth of the population of Ireland and the Scottish Highlands after the introduction of the potato as the staple food of

[1] *Wealth of Nations*, bk. iii. ch. iv.

the people; and another proof is afforded by the increase of the number of marriages as corn falls in price. But it is by no means necessary that a decreased cost in the production of food should be followed by a corresponding increase in population; agricultural produce may be used to feed other animals as well as man; the use of domestic animals may increase, and there may be an increased consumption of agricultural luxuries; and everything tends to show that in the progress of society the "standard of wretchedness" tends to rise, and preventive to be substituted for positive checks. Accordingly, so far as the pressure of population is concerned, it is quite possible that in the future "economic rents" will tend to fall, and a Government speculating for the rise in "unearned increments" on this ground alone might make a serious mistake, especially if the probable appreciation of gold be taken into account. (*Cf.* Ch. XII.)

The famous paradox of Ricardo that improvements tend in the first place to lower rent is not always true even theoretically, and applied to "economic" rent in the strictest sense. Ricardo's argument runs as follows: "In a country which produces its own food the immediate effect of a sudden improvement in the arts of cultivation [supposed to be universally adopted] would be to lower the price of agricultural produce, to make it unprofitable to apply so much capital as before to good land, and to throw some land out of cultivation."[1] Rents reckoned in produce in this case might and probably would fall (as Ricardo and Mill argue), but they might also rise. It is beyond the scope of this work to solve the problem generally, but there can be little doubt that the fall in price would in time be partly, if not wholly, regained, and landlords' rents rise above what they were before. And this leads us to observe that the main cause of the increase of landlord's rent (or the total rent paid by any piece of land) is the increase of agricultural skill and the embodiment of permanent improvements in the soil, and not the resort to inferior soil nor the diminishing return per unit of capital. Precisely the same amount of land might remain in cultivation, and the produce due to the last unit of capital applied might remain constant, and yet rents might be continually rising. How much of the rent due to a *general* improvement is unearned, and how much should be surrendered to the tenants or to the public, I will not profess to determine.

[1] Marshall's *Economics of Industry*, p. 85.

CHAPTER VII.

THE NATIONALISATION OF LAND.

"The land shall not be sold for ever: for the land is Mine; for ye are strangers and sojourners with Me."—LEVITICUS xxv. 23.

THE nationalisation of the land is advocated on a variety of grounds by different individuals; it is maintained that the land belongs of right to the people, that Government would manage it better than the present race of landlords, that it would be a good investment for the State, owing to the prospect of large unearned increments, and that the State has a right to these increments without payment on giving one or two centuries' notice of its intention to appropriate them. The schemes for effecting the proposed nationalisation may be divided into two groups, according as they propose to give compensation to the present owners or not; the former have the greater appearance of justice, the latter of simplicity. The degree of compensation suggested also varies from the full market value (including the capitalised value of the future rise in price, and also the *pretium affectionis* due to social considerations), down to an annuity of the present rental to the present owner, and to his heir or nominee.

The objections to the purchase by Government of the land at its full market value are obvious: the *pretium affectionis* would bring no equivalent, and the value of the future rise might never be recouped; it is quite possible in this country that rents may not rise, and may even fall, for a considerable time, even if there is no appreciation of gold, an event which seems more than probable. But anything less than full compensation would imply the greatest social revolution of modern times, and would shake to its foundations the whole system of private property; for the unearned increment is by no means confined to rent, as a glance at any share list at once reveals, and the Socialists of the Continent consider the greater part of profits as unearned and a proper subject for confiscation. Some writers, indeed, have supposed that by a judicious use of "time," which certainly costs nothing, adequate compensation might be given at a very small real cost. It has been proposed that the land should become the property of the State after one or more centuries, the State paying for it, so to speak, by instalments. It has been calculated by Professor Marshall that supposing the payments were made by the remission of taxes falling on rent, due compensation for the reversion of the title-deeds would be as follows: "Assume the gross rental of land to be 3 per cent. on its value—then, supposing the value of land to double in a hundred years, the reversion of its title-deeds at the end of that time would be compensated by the immediate remission of taxes, amounting to 1*s.* 8*d.* in the pound on rental, taking interest at three per cent.; but only 10*d.* in the pound if we take interest at 4 per cent. If we suppose that the price of land a hundred years hence will be the same as now, the compensation would be 1*s.* in the pound, taking interest at 3 per per cent.; but only 6*d.* taking it at 4 per cent. The State then might offer to remit, say, 1*s.* on the pound on the rent of all land the title-deeds of which due one hundred years hence were transferred to the State." The burden to be distributed over the remainder of the public does not seem very heavy, but the question is naturally suggested, whether it would not be advisable to pay off the National Debt in some similar way before purchasing the land; for if there is a serious appreciation of gold, the sooner the National Debt is paid off, and the longer the valuation of the land is deferred, the more the nation will gain.

The scheme for the nationalisation of the land without compensation which has attracted most attention in recent years is that propounded by Mr. Henry George in his work entitled *Progress and*

Poverty, which has caused a good deal of sensation amongst people not very well read in socialistic literature. The book contains nothing new—even the style appears to be modelled on that of writers of the French Revolutionary era; but as it has achieved a great success, and forms an excellent source of inspiration for advocates of the nationalisation of land, it seems to demand some examination in a work like the present. The main, if not the sole object of Mr. George is to prove that the abolition of private rent would effect the abolition of poverty at the same time. The corner-stone of Mr. George's wonderful edifice is the "unearned increment" from land—the "economic rent" of Ricardo, which seems to have the same effect on the balance of the judgment of those who wish to nationalise the land as compound interest and sinking funds have on those who propose to pay off the National Debt;—invest a penny at compound interest, and in a few centuries the thing is done.

Mr. George sees clearly that Mill's scheme for buying up the land with liberal compensation to its present owners, "even at something above the market value," although it might do no harm, could certainly do no good, because the present value includes the future expectation, and the action of Government would be purely speculative, and accordingly he proposes to seize the land without compensation, or at any rate with only a small portion of compensation. But the obvious difficulty is presented: How will Government manage the land? The answer[1] is remarkable for its simplicity: "Nor to take rent for public purposes, is it necessary that the State should bother with the letting of lands, and assume the chances of the favouritism, collusion, and corruption that might involve." The machinery already exists—all that is necessary is to leave the landlords a percentage of the rent, "probably much less than the cost and loss involved in attempting to rent lands through State agency"—that is to say, reduce the landlord to the position of a badly-paid land-agent, and allow him the nominal title of owner, and he will perform all the functions of a good landlord just as well as before.

Generally, however, Mr. George seems to be impressed by the justice of leaving to a landowner that part of the rent due to his own capital and labour, and proposes only to touch the economic rent due to the "natural and indestructible" powers of the soil. The whole of this he proposes to absorb by taxation, and the best answer to his proposal is to show that if carried out in the most successful manner, it could not have the effects contemplated—at any rate in this country, and as the rental of old is higher than that of new countries, presumably in no other country. The rental of agricultural lands in the United Kingdom may be taken as about £67,000,000. The

[1] Page 364.

amount of revenue raised by imperial taxation is about £69,000,000, and by local taxation about £37,000,000—that is, a total revenue from taxation of about £106,000,000. It appears, then, that if Government took the whole rental of land, the revenue (imperial and local — for both cannot get the rent) would require to be supplemented by £30,000,000 to £40,000,000 of taxes. Yet Mr. George is bold enough to say: "In every civilised country, even the newest, the value of the land taken as a whole is sufficient to bear the entire expenses of Government." But the case is still stronger against Mr. George if he only takes the "economic rent," and to determine how much of the £67,000,000 of gross rental is "economic," would afford him a good introduction to the study of history and statistics.

But the worst still remains. Mr. George disposes of the remedies for low wages that have recommended themselves to working men, to economists, and to legislators in two dozen out of the forty-two dozen pages in which his own remedy is presented to the world; greater economy in government, education, combinations, co-operation, Government assistance, the more general distribution of land—all or any of them are of no avail. Instead of these miserable make-shifts, observe what a prospect is opened up in the following passage: "What I therefore propose as the simple yet sovereign remedy which will raise wages, increase the earnings of capital, extirpate pauperism, abolish poverty, give remunerative employment to whoever wishes it, afford free scope to human powers, lessen crime, elevate morals and taste and intelligence, purify government, and carry civilisation to yet nobler heights is—*to appropriate rent by taxation*."[1] There is no injustice, for "it is not necessary to confiscate land, it is only necessary to confiscate rent." But if this means anything, it means that the present system of taxation is the cause of all the ills of society, which an analysis of the revenue seems very far from confirming.

Of the revenue of this country we find that the customs duties on spirits, tobacco, and wine yield about £18,000,000, and the excise duties on beer and spirits about £24,000,000, per annum. Thus drink and tobacco bear £42,000,000 of the taxation, and it is hardly likely that the "economic rent" could exceed this sum, so that the regeneration of mankind is to be accomplished by seizing the incomes of the landlords, and giving the working man cheap beer, spirits, tobacco, and tea, for these are the only taxes which fall on him to any appreciable extent. But the *reductio ad absurdum* is reached if we consider what effect it would have on the prosperity of the working classes if the whole rental ("economic" and all other) were divided amongst them, at the same time freeing them from all taxation. The working

[1] Page 364.

classes form (roughly speaking) two-thirds of the total population of the British Isles—we may suppose they number about twenty-five millions—and the gross rental (including ground rents) may be estimated at £75,000,000—so that £3 per head per annum would be the result of the direct distribution of the rents—truly a small sum by which to regenerate society.

Mr. George does not seem to be aware that the experiment of absorbing the rent for the benefit of the poor was actually tried in England at the commencement of this century. It is true the experiment was only partially carried out; it was only in a few instances the poor-rates absorbed the whole of the rent; still at that time the distinction between "economic" and "profit" rent had only been revealed to the few, and it is quite possible that the whole of the former was absorbed. The direct object of the taxation was to raise wages to the natural level; but the experiment failed, and the country nearly failed also. Whether in a new country Government should retain the ownership of the land and only let the usufruct, is an important practical problem, which, however, lies beyond the scope of the present work.

CHAPTER VIII.

THE CAUSES WHICH DETERMINE THE FAIR RENT OF LAND.

"The rent of land corresponds to the price of goods, but doubtless was infinitely slower in conforming to economical law, since the impression of a brotherhood in the ownership of land still survived when goods had long since become the subject of individual property. . . . . What is sometimes called the feudal feeling has much in common with the old feeling of brotherhood, which forbade hard bargains, though, like much else, it has passed from the collective community to the modern representative of its autocratic chieftain."—*Village Communities.* SIR HENRY S. MAINE.

WHATEVER opinion is held concerning the theoretical value of Ricardo's doctrine of Rent, it must, I think, be admitted that it is too abstract to be of practical utility. The rents which should be paid in Great Britain depend on a number of variable causes, which it is impossible to bring in merely as modifications of the law of diminishing returns. These causes fall naturally into three groups, according as they affect (*a*) the amount of the produce, (*b*) the price of that produce, and (*c*) the expenses of production.

(*a*) *Causes affecting the amount of the produce.*—The recent agricultural depression has made abundantly clear that over the period of the average duration of a lease the most important factor in determining the amount of the produce is the state of the seasons, and it seems equally clear that even nineteen years is not sufficiently long to ensure an "average" crop. No one who entered on a lease ten years ago could have foreseen the seasons which were to follow, and but for the natural persistence of good old customs, the lease system would have received its death-blow. Next in importance to the seasons, as affecting the amount of the produce, is the security for the investment of capital by the tenant. Even that extent of security afforded by a nineteen years lease has made Scotch farming, in the opinion of the best authorities, the most productive in the world. The advantage of such security is shown as much by the faults as by the merits of the lease system.[1] It is well known that as the lease approaches its close the farmer, in the natural and undisguised endeavour to get back as much of his capital as possible, takes so much out of the land that for some years after the yield is considerably reduced. The extraordinary improvements effected by peasant proprietors must also

[1] See below, p. 111.

be principally ascribed to the security afforded by ownership.

Another cause of primary importance in determining the amount of the produce is the energy and skill of the farmer.[1] Perhaps the best illustration of this is to be found in the fact that large estates farmed under a system of delegated management are not nearly so productive as when let to tenant farmers. There is nothing a large proprietor dislikes so much as having farms thrown on his hands. Again, it has often been asserted that there is at present a good opening for Scotch farmers in the Midlands of England, on farms which have been abandoned by the less skilful Southerner. Agriculture, too, is rapidly becoming more dependent on science and technical training. A farmer, for example, who does not understand the composition of the artificial manures he uses, and who does not know, except by hearsay, the effects of the different ingredients, cannot obtain so much from his land as the man who has carefully studied these matters, and it would be easy to extend the list of scientific requirements. In connection with agricultural skill, "freedom of cropping" ought to be mentioned, taking the term in its widest sense; for there can be no doubt that in many cases land is less productive than it might be, owing to restrictions placed on the enterprise of the

[1] An Aberdonian, it is said, can pay 30 per cent. more rent for his land than the average British farmer could afford.

farmer as regards the kind of crop. The efficiency of the labourers must also operate largely, and it appears from the Report of the Agricultural Commission that farmers have suffered by the deterioration of agricultural labour. This may be easily accounted for by the increasing emigration of the better members of that class, owing to the higher rate of wages and the greater chance of success in manufacturing industries. Another illustration is afforded by the slovenly work performed under the old system of poor relief. In some cases production is checked by want of capital on the part of the tenant, and this is one of the principal arguments against the laws of distress and hypothec. It is said that the landlord, knowing himself to be secure, takes a tenant without sufficient capital, and the tenant is unable to borrow, owing to the preferential claim of the landlord. Again, it can hardly be doubted that the want of capital is one of the chief causes of the comparative unproductiveness of Irish agriculture.

(*b*) *Causes affecting the price of the produce.*—The second group of causes determining rent consists of those which affect the prices obtained for the produce. Changes in price may occur either owing to some change in the standard of value, or to changes in the demand and supply or in the conditions of production, of agricultural commodities. It is unnecessary at this point[1] to enumerate the various causes which may affect prices generally—the rate

[1] See Chap. XII.

of production of the precious metals, the economies in their use, the expansion or contraction of trade, changes in the currency of nations, etc.—but it may be asserted with some confidence that the course of general prices for the next nineteen years is as uncertain and indeterminate as the course of the seasons. It has been estimated that in England 99½ per cent. of commercial transactions are completed without the intervention of money, and much further economy in the use of bullion seems hardly possible. Yet, at the same time, this gigantic credit system has for its foundation the ½ per cent. of bullion; if a few millions were withdrawn from the Bank of England, the whole structure would totter or collapse. Whilst this is the case in England and in the more populous and civilised parts of America, in the Western States, on the other hand, there is an increasing demand for bullion. It is possible that America, if its trade and population increase as rapidly as they have done during this century, may for the future absorb gold as steadily as India does silver.[1] In the sixteenth century English agriculture was seriously affected by the amount of treasure brought from the New World; the general rise in prices consequent on the increase of the precious metals began with those commodities which were most marketable, and only slowly extended over the articles which did not naturally find their way into the general markets of the country. It is

[1] See Chap. XII.

quite possible that the absorption of the precious metals by America and our Colonies may lead to results of a converse kind. If a general fall of prices occurs before the end of the century, the commodities first affected will, no doubt, be manufactures; but wages tend more and more to follow the course of prices in manufacturing industries, and a general fall in wages will immediately lead to a fall in the price of agricultural luxuries (meat, etc.). If such an event occurs, the farmer obviously cannot at once recoup himself by the diminished expenses of labour. It is sometimes assumed that any cause which affects prices in general makes no difference in relative values; and it may be supposed that the farmer will gain with one hand what he loses with the other. But although the assumption is correct when equilibrium has been attained, the passage from one level of prices to another is, as a matter of fact, accompanied by very great disturbances of relative values. Many more arguments might be brought forward in support of the contention that for nineteen, or even for ten years the course of general prices is indeterminate, and that a change in general prices will disturb the relative values of agricultural produce; but enough has been said to illustrate the extreme uncertainty of the prices the farmer will obtain, even when we take into account only the causes which affect the value of commodities in general. But this uncertainty becomes still greater when we take into consideration the causes which affect agricultural prices specially. As far as corn is concerned, it may be maintained that its price will for many years be determined by its cost of production in America or our Colonies. The supplies we receive from abroad form such a large proportion of the total amount consumed (about one-half), that any falling-off in the importations would be immediately followed by a rise in price. It will be remembered that on the outbreak of the war between Turkey and Russia the price of the quartern loaf was raised one penny on account of the anticipated check to the Russian trade, and it is noteworthy that, in spite of the great deficiency of the home harvests during the recent depression, the price of corn was not affected, owing to the enormous supplies from America. It may be anticipated that, in spite of the rapid growth of population in the New World and the Colonies, a long period must elapse before the point of diminishing return is reached. There are still vast tracts of country to be brought under the plough, and when all the land has been put under cultivation it has still to be subjected to the serious operation of high farming, in place of the "tickling" practised at present. As soon as high farming becomes profitable, the settlers on the new lands can avail themselves of all the arts of the Old World. There can be little doubt then that for a considerable period the cost of production abroad will determine the price of corn in this country. But whether this cost of production is likely to rise or fall can hardly be conjectured. The cost of transport will probably diminish, and the rate of profit may possibly fall; but, on the other hand, the cost of labour may rise, and, when the virgin soil is exhausted, manures must be used. Again, if America adopts free trade, an enormous stimulus will be given to agriculture, and a still further fall in the price of corn ensue, for free trade may be expected to lower the price of corn in America in the same way as it lowered the price of manufactures in our own country. The prices of meat and dairy produce, in so far as independent of the price of corn, do not seem at present to be quite so much under the influence of foreign competition. Apart from the difficulties of transport the quality of the article has to be considered, and as far as the better qualities are concerned competition is not so much to be feared. Still there can be no doubt that the foreign supply will increase, and it is quite possible that English mutton may follow the example of English wool. It is clear, then, that the kind of crop is an important element in determining rent.

(c) *Causes affecting the expenses of production.*—The third group of causes which operate on rent consists of the factors which enter into the expenses of production. One of the most important is the cost of labour. It may, I think, be anticipated that the rate of agricultural wages will for some time continue to rise relatively to other wages. The spread of education will inevitably increase the number of emigrants, and we may expect the best agricultural labourers to go to the Colonies, where their peculiar qualifications are most in request. Hence, probably, labour will both become dearer and less efficient; and the report of the late Commission shows that these effects have already commenced.

Immigration to the towns operates as powerfully in the same direction as emigration from the country. It has long been a subject of remark that the rate of agricultural wages is always higher in the neighbourhood of large towns, and the conjecture may be hazarded, that with increased knowledge and increased facilities of communication, agricultural wages may at no distant date rank higher than the rate in most manufactures. If such an event takes place, no doubt encouragement will be given to substitutive machinery, but such machinery will require greater skill in its manipulation, and wages may rise still higher. The other elements of expense involve technical rather than economic considerations, but perhaps the opinion may be expressed that the cost of machinery will tend to fall and the price of manures to rise.

There is, however, still one element affecting rent to be taken into account which, logically, should be classed with expenses, and that is—farmers' profits. Under a system of competition rents, where farming is, like any other business, carried on for profit, the usual rate of profit is as much part of the expenses as the usual rate of wages. If education and increased facilities of communication tend to increase the emigration of labour, still more will they increase the emigration of the farmer and his capital. The number of British farmers who have emigrated during the last ten years is very considerable, and would, no doubt, have been greatly increased, but for the system of leases. Landlords cannot expect farmers to go on cultivating their land if they are to obtain little or no profit. In determining a "fair" rent, then, the rate of profit is an important factor.

It follows, from the variety of causes considered, and the number might have been easily increased, that a "fair" rent is a surplus which is uncertain and indeterminate. The popular notion, probably founded on the tradition of customary rents, and in England on the fact that land was until recently generally undervalued, that for every farm there is a certain "natural" rent, which a "practical" man can easily determine from the quality of the soil, the state of the drains, etc., must be abandoned. The relative value of two farms, as instruments of production, the practical men may, no doubt, readily determine, but the fair letting value, for a long term of years, requires many more, and more complex considerations to be taken into account. The practical man certainly shot very wide of the mark ten years ago. The persistence of the notion is very well illustrated by the fact that the proposal to fix rents in Ireland for a term of *fifteen* years met with very little opposition. It is to be hoped, on political and social grounds, that the Commissioners have left a considerable margin in favour of the tenant.

As an illustration of the difficulty of determining rent, I give a table from the Appendix to Sir James Caird's *Landed Interest*, which shows the average rent of cultivated land per acre at three different periods, and some of the principal elements which affect rent.

TABLE showing the Rent of Cultivated Land, the Price of Provisions, the Wages of the Agricultural Labourer, the Rent of Cottages, and the average Produce of Wheat, in three periods, during the last hundred years in England.

	1770.		1850.		1878.	
	s.	*d.*	*s.*	*d.*	*s.*	*d.*
Rent of Cultivated Land per acre, . . .	13	0	27	0	30	0
Price of Bread per lb., .	0	1½	0	1¼	0	1½
,, Meat ,, . .	0	3¼	0	5	0	9
,, Butter ,, . .	0	6	1	0	1	8
Agricultural Labourer's Wages per week, . .	7	3	9	7	14	0
Rent of Labourer's Cottage per week, . . .	0	8	1	5	2	0
Produce of Wheat per acre in bushels, . . .	Bushels. 23		Bushels. 26½		Bushels. 28	

Now how can the fact that between 1770 and 1878 rent was more than doubled be explained? The yield per acre has indeed increased, but *per contra*, the rate of wages has been almost doubled; again, the price of bread is the same, whilst meat and butter have risen to nearly three times their former value. As far as the facts in the table indicate, the causes of the rise in rent appear to be the increased productiveness of the soil, and the great rise in the price of other kinds of produce than corn. But the problem could not be fully solved without bringing in other elements, *e.g.* the relative amounts of taxation incident on land, the rates of profit current at the two periods, the cost of carriage of materials, and products, etc. We should further have to take into account the course of seasons in the years preceding, and the course of prices. It would have to be considered also how far in the former period rents were customary, and how far in the latter they were really competition rents. And after making all allowances, it would be well to compare the corresponding rise in Belgium, and especially in France, where there has been no increase in population.

CHAPTER IX.

THE METHODS OF DETERMINING FAIR RENTS, AND HOW FAR GOVERNMENT INTERFERENCE IS DESIRABLE.

"The three rents are rack-rent, from a person of a strange tribe—a fair rent, from one of the tribe—and the stipulated rent, which is paid equally by the tribe and the strange tribe." SENCHUS MOR.

IN the last chapter the various considerations which govern fair rents were examined, and it is at once clear that an accurate determination, for practical purposes, must be very difficult, owing to the complexity and uncertainty of the causes affecting price, the amount of produce, and the expenses of production.

The next problem is to investigate the best practical method for surmounting these difficulties, and to consider how far the assistance of Government is required. But apart from the real difficulty of determining a fair rent, even supposing both landlord and tenant can estimate the factors indicated with sufficient accuracy for practical purposes, the preliminary question arises, Whether the contracting parties are on an equal footing? In making any bargain it seldom happens that the position of the parties is equally favourable for obtaining a fair result, and where the inequality is great, a case often arises for Government interference. The most obvious example is furnished by monopolies. Where there is no competition, the owner of a monopolised article can fix any prices he may please. If a railway has the monopoly of a district, the inhabitants are at the mercy of the company, and the company may have different rates for different individuals. Without multiplying examples, it may be said that, in nearly every case of monopoly, it might be desirable for Government to interfere in the interests of the public. It is often urged that the landowners of a country have a monopoly, and can, therefore, drive unfair bargains with their tenants, and indirectly injure the public. In support of this contention, it is said that land is limited, and no doubt this is true: but limitation is an essential quality in all wealth; whenever the supply of a commodity is unlimited, its value is *nil.* But the essence of monopoly is not limitation, but absence of competition. If all the land of this country were held by one individual, or by a group acting in combination, then rents might reach an unfair and injurious height. But no one can deny that there is sufficient competition amongst the owners of land to invalidate the charge of monopoly in the ordinary sense. Sometimes, however, when the monopoly of land is spoken of, what is really meant is the general statement that the landowner is in a better position than the tenant to make a bargain. There may be a country where the population is excessive and mainly rural—there may be what is termed land-hunger—there may be more tenants than there are holdings, and the want of a holding may mean starvation, or emigration, which is dreaded almost as much. In this case high authority may be brought forward in favour of Government valuation; the principle has been adopted in the recent Irish legislation, and is now being advocated as the best solution of the Highland crofter difficulty. But it may be questioned if the fundamental evil in land-hunger is rack-renting. Nothing can be more certain than that, where minute subdivision of the soil exists, the fair rent is something below zero, for the produce will not even give fair wages of labour; and it may be doubted, where the holdings are sufficiently large, if rack-renting has ever been such as to justify Government interference. No peasantry are more rack-rented than those of Flanders,[1] and, perhaps, none are more prosperous. It may be answered that the increased size of the holding is of no consequence if the competition of

Compare the Essay by E. de Laveleye, on the Land Systems of Belgium and Holland in *Systems of Land Tenure in Various Countries* (Cobden Club).

tenants forces up the rent to such a pitch that the occupier will have no more left than before. But if compensation for improvements were secured, and a fair notice of removal given, a tenant,[1] though rack-rented at first, would soon escape from his bondage. Give the crofter sufficient field for his labour, and secure to him the fruits of his labour, and further interference of Government would not be required.

But at any rate the farmers of Great Britain above the crofter class cannot raise the plea of rack-renting on account of land-hunger. Sometimes, however, the intervention of Government in fixing rents is demanded on other grounds, and other reasons are given to show that in making a contract landlord and tenant are not on an equal footing. It is said that the tenant will often consent to an addition to his rent rather than quit his holding, and will give what is tantamount to a *pretium affectionis.* Again, it is maintained that the law of distress unduly increases competition; that incompetent men offer more than the subject is worth, and that thereby average rents are unfairly raised. If the landlord is changed by sale of the land, or by the death or incapacity of the first lessor, the lessee has, under the present law, no power to break his lease, although he may consider that his new landlord (*e.g.* from sporting or social considerations, unwillingness to advance capital, etc.) is not worth so much as his predecessor. On the

[1] See next chapter.

other hand, however, it must be allowed that the landowner cannot as a rule farm his own land profitably, and so far the tenant has the advantage in making the bargain. On the whole, so far as the relative position of the contracting parties is concerned, it appears that if all preferential laws were removed, there would be no ground for Government intervention in fixing rents. If security of tenure and security for the investment of capital were possible only with leases having a fixed rent for long periods, then perhaps circumstances might arise in which Government might advantageously intervene; but there is no necessary connection between fixity of tenure and fixity of rent, nor between either of them and security for the investment of capital.[1] Besides, those who complain of seasons and prices below the worst they anticipated—worse than any one could have anticipated—and therefore demand compulsory remission of rent, would be very unwilling to submit to the converse operation in years of unprecedented and unexpected prosperity.

As regards the actual difficulties in calculating a fair rent, owing to the variable causes enumerated in the last chapter, on which a fair rent depends, a Government official would not be, or ought not to be, in any better position than the parties interested. Government cannot foresee the seasons, the prices, and the expenses any better than private individuals.

[1] *Cf.* next chapter.

But there is one thing Government can and ought to do, to which private enterprise is unequal. Statistics and information on all matters pertaining to agriculture in this and other countries ought to be compiled with due speed and accuracy, so that those interested may be in a position to form a better opinion on agricultural prospects.

There can be no doubt that one of the first effects of the reform of the land laws will be to cause land to be let more and more on commercial principles. With the remnants of feudal privilege will be driven away the remnants of feudal obligation. In Ireland the introduction of the commercial principle had the effect of new wine in old bottles, and even in Great Britain, if disasters are to be avoided, contracts for the hire of land can no longer rest on the old rule of thumb. If "free trade" in land produces the effects its advocates anticipate, we shall have in many cases commercial landlords exacting commercial rents. But at present it may be safely said that most tenant farmers have no conception of the causes which determine the prices on which their whole fortunes depend, and they rival the gambler or the gold-digger in their belief in good seasons. To some extent the same cause which renders a lottery a success for its promoters, and the reverse on the average to the buyers of tickets, accounts for the low rate of farming profits. The same principle is illustrated in the fact brought out by Mr. Nash, in his work on the "Profitable Nature of our Investments," that the investments of the last ten years have paid this country almost inversely as the risk involved.

One can never know that a turn of good seasons and high prices is not to come round—a war may break out with America, or the sun may change its spots;—and farmers continually risk their all and more than their all in what is practically a speculation for the rise. Again, agriculture has always been considered the most delightful of all occupations, and the "agreeableness of the employment"[1] also tends to lower the rate of profit. But when the margin of profit is so narrow, the amount of rent is an important element. It is worth observing that whilst according to the teaching of economists ordinary farming profits should equitably be a first charge on the produce and rent a varying surplus, the very reverse is followed in practice—rent is fixed and profits vary. So long as this fixed rent was considerably below the competition rent, the difference being made up to the landlord on social considerations, the only effect was that agriculture was conducted (like any other industry that receives a bounty) in a slovenly manner, customary rents being generally found with customary cultivation. But if competition rents are to be introduced, the tenant must consider the extreme variations to which such rents

[1] *Cf.* Adam Smith, bk. i. ch. 10.

(if "fair") are subject. At the present time the farmer looks on land as his raw material to which he applies his labour and capital to manufacture mutton, corn, etc. He regards the rent as the price paid for this raw material; and he thinks he is no worse off than any other manufacturer in paying for it before he knows at what price he can sell the produce. But, in the first place, no manufacturer would undertake to give the same price for his raw material for twenty years, and secondly, the movements of wages, the other principal element in cost, follow the movements of prices;—in manufactures, if the price of the article falls, the wages of the labour fall;—if they do not fall in accordance with a sliding scale already provided, they fall through the action of demand and supply. But it was pointed out in the last chapter that the cost of agricultural labour is, at present, much affected by causes independent of agriculture, and that the cost will probably rise. If the economic mode of regarding rent be correct, the farmer should be compensated by a corresponding fall in rent; but if he enters on a long lease, he is debarred from this relief. He should also find some relief in reduced rent, if prices fall or the seasons are unfavourable;—but the long lease possesses no elasticity. It seems desirable then to examine how far rents, which vary according to some sliding scale, are advantageous and practicable. Of the advantage theoretically there can be no doubt.

During the recent depression much farming capital was absorbed in the payment of high rents, and the consequent bankruptcy of many farmers gave a check to agricultural production, from which the community at large suffered. And if the contrary case arises, and, owing to exceptional seasons or prices, leaseholders make uncommon profits, the inevitable effect is an extreme rise in rent after the event, and when it is no longer justified, and the period of inflation is again followed by depression.

If a sliding scale were adopted, it might be constructed either in the roughest and simplest or in the most complex manner; it might only come into operation when great changes took place, or it might produce changes in rents according to the smallest fluctuations of the variable causes. A very simple case, perhaps the simplest possible, is furnished by the Code Napoléon. Whenever the deficiency of the crop exceeds one-half of an average harvest, the landlord is obliged to share in the loss; but his interest is protected, when the land is let for a term of years, by the provision that the tenant must prove a loss of more than half the ordinary crop over the whole period, taking both good and bad years into account. The ground of the landlord's liability is that he is bound to furnish a "*possession utile,*" and his claim for rent depends on the land fulfilling the purposes for which it was let. In the case just considered, the sliding scale only comes into operation in very exceptional circumstances.

There is, however, a mode of paying rents, which still prevails in some parts of Southern Europe, in which the principle of the sliding scale (according to produce) is fully adopted; that is in what is known as the Métayer system. Under this system the landlord provides both the land and the capital, and in return receives half the produce. The objections are obvious. Adam Smith pointed out that the tithe, which only took a tenth of the gross produce, acted as a powerful drag on the energy of the farmer, and experience shows that the same objection applies to the Métayer system. In fact both theory and practice confirm the opinion that produce rents, pure and simple, in which the landlord actually obtains a share of the proceeds of his particular piece of land, are economically disadvantageous. They lead to slovenly cultivation and want of enterprise, for the tenant knows that the results of any special skill or effort must be shared by another. There are also great practical difficulties in the payment of kind, or, if that is avoided, in estimating the value of the produce, and produce rents have always tended to disappear before money rents, thus proving the latter to be the fittest to survive.

Sometimes the other important element in the "fair" rent—the course of prices—has been taken as the foundation of a sliding scale. Until quite recent times,[1] many farms were let in Scotland on rents varying with the "fiars' prices," which may be roughly described as the average prices of grain, in a certain district, for a certain period. I am not aware of any attempt having been made to make rents vary according to the third principal element, the expenses of production, although theoretically the average wages of labour, cost of materials, etc., are as well fitted as prices and seasons to enter into a sliding scale for rent. In favour of a sliding scale it may be argued that the remissions of rent, which have been so generally made of late, must have been founded on some principles, and if a sliding scale were adopted, it would only amount to making these principles explicit before and not after some event has occurred. Certain general principles may be laid down—on the analogy of other industries where the sliding scale has worked satisfactorily—which must be followed if the plan is attempted in agriculture. So far as produce is concerned, the basis must be taken on the production of large areas, as shown by official statistics; otherwise a landlord might be defrauded through the negligence and want of skill of the tenant. Again, prices must be average prices, so as to place no check on the enterprise of the tenant in taking advantage of market fluctuations.

The same observations apply to the expenses of

[1] I am informed the practice has not yet entirely ceased.

production. It would never do to make rent in any way depend on the cost incurred on a particular farm.[1] I quote a passage from Professor Marshall's *Economics of Industry,* which explains very clearly other characteristics of a sliding scale: "A sliding scale must not be expected to work for a very long time together without alteration; it must, at all events, be recast whenever any considerable change occurs in the manner of carrying on the trade. The provisions of a sliding scale must be definite and unmistakable, but perhaps more harm than good is done by trying to make them extremely simple. Nature is not simple but complex; and a sliding scale that aims not at resisting, but at guiding the work of natural laws, must sometimes be complex too. Thus it should generally take account not only of the price which the manufacturer gets for his goods, but also of that which he pays for his raw material. For instance, the standard price in the iron trade, instead of being the price of a bar of a certain kind of pig iron, might be the excess of the price over the price of the ironstone and coal that are used in making it. And the standards in the cotton trade should have reference to the price which manufacturers have to pay for their raw cotton as well as to those which they get for their finished goods."[2]

But it seems improbable that sliding-scale rents,

[1] See next chapter. [2] Page 216.

although without doubt the fairest theoretically, except of the roughest type, will ever be adopted in this country. The considerations are too complex for practical purposes if approximate accuracy is looked for; and even if a good scale were constructed, there are practical objections to its use which appear fatal. It takes a view of rent, which, though theoretically the soundest, does not recommend itself to either the British landlord or the British tenant. The landlord wishes to know beforehand precisely what he is to receive, and the tenant makes all his calculations on the basis of a definitely known rent. Under the sliding-scale system the landlord would conceive his income endangered; — up to recent years, land was considered the safest of all investments, and the idea, though erroneous, still prevails;—while the tenant would object to the system on the ground that he preferred a certain amount of risk, and that under its operation, though failure might be minimised, success would be minimised also. Healthy speculation is, after all, the soul of industry, and the mere fact that a farmer has to make up a rent often gives him the energy to do so. The tenant also would naturally fear that the sliding scale would turn his landlord from a sleeping into an active partner. Again, so far as the interests of the community are affected, the nation is much more concerned with the progress of agriculture than with the failure of particular and presumably inferior farmers, for like Nature—

> "So careful of the type she seems,
> So careless of the single life."

But if a sliding scale is found impossible or disagreeable, another alternative presents itself, in fixing rents for much shorter periods than the nineteen years of the common Scotch lease; although landlords who wish to have a fixed income, and tenants who believe in their good fortune, and members of both classes who have a vague impression that nineteen years is a period adapted to secure an average price for an average crop, will no doubt still adhere to the old system. It is, of course, possible that a series of fortunate coincidences may satisfy the expectations of both classes, just as it is possible, if a man agreed to buy pig-iron every New Year's Day at a fixed price for twenty years, he might come out of the experiment with the ordinary rate of profit on his capital. The great objection to shorter periods (say five years) for rents is founded on the confusion already noticed, that the period for which a rent is fixed must determine the period of the tenancy. But it is easy to see that nineteen or twenty years (which would suit the five-year system of rotation) might be retained as the length of the tenancy, and yet the rent be changed several times during that period. The rent, for example, might be periodically determined by arbitration (which every day becomes of more and more importance in every branch of industry), if landlord and tenant could not otherwise come to an agreement; or the basis of any change might be clearly laid down at the commencement of the lease. Under the present system leases are often granted with rents which are smaller at the commencement than subsequently, on the grounds apparently of extra expense being anticipated in the first years, and extra produce in the later period.

But whatever method of fixing fair rents is resorted to, two things are abundantly clear: (1) The intervention of Government is not necessary; such intervention checks the "tendency to variation," which is the primary condition of economic as of all other development. There is no more justification for Government fixing rents than for its fixing wages and profits. As soon as the parties interested once grasp the idea that rent depends on a number of variable elements, and that "natural" rent, except in the shape of a low customary rent, is a myth, necessity may be relied on for inventing some appropriate method of calculation. (2) The indirect advantages of the long-lease system, in giving partial fixity of tenure and security for tenant's capital, have, as the agriculture of Scotland shows, been so great, that if, owing to the possible causes of variation, rent comes to be fixed for a short period only, it is absolutely necessary in the interests of landlord, tenant, and consumer alike, that some method should be arrived at for securing these important benefits of the lease. Unless security be afforded against sudden or arbitrary eviction, and for the investment of capital and the freedom of enterprise, it may be considered certain that the Scotch farmer will prefer to retain the lease system, with all its risks and disadvantages.

CHAPTER X.

OF FIXITY OF TENURE AND SECURITY FOR THE CAPITAL NECESSARY FOR GOOD HUSBANDRY.

"Inædificatum solo cedit solo."

It was pointed out at the conclusion of the last chapter that if rent, owing to the fluctuating causes on which it depends, is in future fixed for shorter periods than the nineteen years usual in leases in Scotland, it will be necessary to secure in some other way the other two advantages of the long lease—Reasonable Fixity of Tenure and Security for Tenant's Capital. It must be pointed out, however, that these advantages were only partially secured by the long-lease system, partly owing to the state of the land and partly to the usual mode of drawing leases.

(1.) As regards Fixity of Tenure, no doubt during a period of prosperity the tenant was enabled to make large profits and act in an enterprising way; but even then he had no power of assigning or transferring his lease, whilst on the other hand, *nolens volens*, he might be handed over to another landlord—a lease-holder was *ascriptus glebæ;* and it must be remembered that however carefully a lease is drawn, the tenant must in many ways rely on his landlord. In the course of time, however, there is no doubt that the tenant will be placed on the same legal footing as the owner of land, and this artificial objection to leases would disappear. But in periods of depression, especially if the lease had been entered on during an inflated period, the fixity of the tenure for so long a period was an evil; the tenant had no means of escape from a position in which he was being gradually ruined.

Nor was the fixity of tenure for so long a time, although relatively advantageous to the landlord, altogether without its disadvantages. In the period of prosperity he would see the value of land rising without obtaining any share in the rise. Again, the land might be let to a tenant who, altogether apart from social considerations, might prove obnoxious to the landlord on account of his slovenly cultivation. In the period of depression the landlord was no doubt protected to some extent by the preferential laws of distress and hypothec,[1] but he always ran the risk of having the farm suddenly thrown on his hands through the bankruptcy of the tenant. The landlord then, under the long-lease system, might fairly argue that the advantages were not always on his side.

[1] Hypothec was abolished in 1880, but its place is practically taken by the Act of Sederunt.

But if this system is abandoned, it does not seem very difficult to provide for reasonable fixity of tenure. There is the method of periodical re-valuation at stated intervals, the tenancy being for any length that may be desired, and there is the method of giving the tenant the option of breaking the lease at specified times. But the former method would involve arbitration, and might induce the tenant to try to depreciate the value of the holding in order to get a lower rent, whilst the second labours under the more serious disadvantage of making the tenant (being uncertain whether he will avail himself of the option or not) hesitate to sink capital in the farm; he may not sink even the amount necessary for good cultivation. A better method then appears to be a long term of notice fixed by law (say two or even three years), the rent being fixed and the holding taken for any period agreeable to the contracting parties. It may, however, be objected that although two years is long enough to make arrangements for the removal of stock and the acquisition of another holding, it is far too short to enable the tenant to invest capital with safety in the land. It is necessary then to consider how such security may be best attained.

(2.) Here again we notice that the Security for Tenant's Capital and encouragement to enterprise were only partially obtained under the long-lease system. The mode of cultivation followed under that system, as may be gathered from the Report of the Agricultural Commissioners, may be described as follows: Six years to get the land into condition by putting capital into it, seven years' farming according to the rules of good husbandry, the tenant treating the land as if he loved it, then six years to take the capital out that was put in in the first six. The tenant cannot be blamed for his conduct in the last period of the lease; even according to the strict equity of Roman law he is only bound to restore the land in the same condition in which he received it, and according to the English and Scotch law of fixtures, that is his only possible method of compensation. There is no doubt, too, that the tenant was actuated also by a motive less laudable but equally natural, viz. the fear of benefiting the landlord without compensation. It is probably true that most tenants would rather lose a pound by not doing something than benefit their landlords to the extent of half-a-crown by doing it. No man likes to assist in making the unearned increments of another, and tenants as well as landlords are influenced by sentiment. Hence, even if the system of long leases is retained, so far as rent and tenure are concerned, it will be advantageous to both landlord and tenant (and indirectly to the public) to provide for the security of the tenant's capital, and to give him some simpler and less injurious method of recovering his property which has become entangled with that of his landlord. But if the period of tenure is shortened this is still more evident, for otherwise not enough capital may be put into the land for good cultivation, to say nothing of improvements.

As regards security of tenant's capital, experience has clearly shown that it is not sufficient to trust to freedom of contract alone. Of this the most recent proof is furnished by the Agricultural Holdings Act of 1875, which was rendered practically inoperative by the insertion of a permissive clause enabling the parties to contract themselves out of its provisions. It may or may not have been a satisfactory Act otherwise, but at any rate it was supposed to be so, and at present one of the most widely accepted proposals for securing compensation for unexhausted improvements, is to render the provisions of the Act, or the greater part of them, compulsory. The Commissioners on Agriculture state in their Report: "Upon the most careful consideration of the evidence before us, we have arrived at the conclusion that further legislative provision should be made for securing to tenants the compensation to which they are equitably entitled in respect of their outlay, and we recommend that the principles of the Agricultural Holdings Act relating to compensation shall be made compulsory in all cases where such compensation is not otherwise provided for." They also point out that "in many cases landlords have not offered, and tenants have omitted to ask for, the fair compensation, which, we believe, it is the interest of both that the tenant should enjoy, and to which we think he is entitled." It is quite clear, then, that neither a good model furnished by the legislature, nor the good example of a few excellent landords and enterprising tenants, is sufficient to induce the large majority of those interested in the hire of land to avail themselves of the freedom of contract they enjoy to provide for compensation. Both landlords and tenants are largely influenced by custom and sentiment. The landlord is often affected by non-agricultural considerations; on large estates the same form of agreement is adopted for all the farms, and smaller landowners are still influenced by the same class feeling, and impose the same restrictions. On the other hand, tenants are ready to accept conditions injurious to their interests, partly because they can expect no better anywhere else, and partly because they are swayed by the traditions inherited from their fathers. Besides this, they do not really expect obnoxious provisions to be put in force. Yet, in general, the great majority both of landlords and tenants wish that agriculture should flourish, and if they "sat down in a cool moment" they would express the hope that no unfair advantage should be given to either party. But in practice both are apt to imagine that the gain of one must necessarily be the loss of the other, just as many people believe that one-sided free trade must of necessity injure the nation by which it is practised. Accordingly Government interference may be justified on the ground of giving effect to the real wishes of both parties, if it can be shown that both would be benefited, for Government can overrule the customs, sentiments, and fallacies which prevent them benefiting themselves. Such interference may also be justified on the more general ground of the paramount importance of good agriculture to the whole community.

The phrase "freedom of contract" is often used in a vague way, which makes it appear more opposed to positive law than is actually the case. But the very essence of a contract lies in the sanction imposed by the law; every legal right on the one side implies a legal obligation on the other.

Again, in every contract there are certain implied clauses. "In no contract, whether dealing with land or any other subject-matter, do the parties express *in extenso* all the rights and obligations which flow from the actual terms of their agreement; the vast majority of such rights and obligations are not expressed in the contract itself, but are annexed to it by the law. Yet they are regarded as implied terms of the contract; and rightly so, because the parties must be taken to have had regard to them when they entered into their contract, and also because they were at liberty (save in specially excepted cases) to have contracted themselves out of them."[1] But in nearly every important sphere of industry the legislature has made certain clauses compulsory, and has prohibited others. This has been illustrated in a former chapter by the Factory Acts, and shipping, banking, mining, education, etc., furnish numberless examples of the beneficial, if not necessary, interference of Government.

But if freedom of contract is not sufficient to ensure security for the investment of a tenant's capital, it is still more obvious that no such security is afforded, or even contemplated, in the existing laws of Scotland and England.

In England, with regard to lessor and lessee, the general rule is that all fixtures belong to the landlord. An agricultural tenant cannot remove buildings erected by himself, even although he thereby leaves the subject in the same state as when he entered on it. But what is or is not a fixture according to English law it is very difficult to determine. "Throughout, the English judges themselves feel the difficulty of ascertaining a governing principle."[2] The law has, indeed, been relaxed partially by the Act of 1851 (14 and 15 Vict. c. 25), and gradually other modifications have been allowed in the interests of trade. Occasionally, too, the tenant is protected by local customs which have been sup-

[1] Richey's *Irish Land Laws*, p. 9.

[2] Hunter, *Law of Landlord and Tenant*, vol. i. p. 299.

ported in the courts, but there is no doubt that the whole law is in a most unsatisfactory state, and in general may be said to give the tenant absolutely no compensation for his unexhausted improvements —"*Inædificatum solo cedit solo.*" The law of Scotland appears to be no more settled than that of England, according to Hunter. "In Scotland there have been comparatively few cases relatively to the doctrine of fixtures, and none directly involving that doctrine as between landlord and tenant in which principle was settled."[1]

The law of distress places the tenant at a still further disadvantage, for it gives the landlord a preferential claim over all the capital on the farm—whether belonging to the tenant or to a third party. It is curious to contrast the care for the landlord's rent with the utter indifference shown by the law to the tenant's capital, and yet in high farming on land (for example) rented at £2 per acre, £14 per

[1] There have been several cases of importance since Hunter wrote. (*Cf.* 4th edition, p. 321.) His editor writes: "The rule is recognised that in leases of ordinary duration, when the tenant erects fixtures solely for the purpose of his trade, these remain his property, and cannot be claimed by the landlord as '*partes soli.*'" It would therefore appear that there is nothing in the principle of the law of Scotland to prevent this rule being applied to agriculture, and the proposals in this chapter amount to no more than a full application to agriculture of the general principle on which the rule is based.

acre may be invested by the tenant, and very often more than the rental be annually applied to the land (in the use of artificial manures, feeding stuffs, etc.).

Those who are never weary of extolling the blessings of "free trade" in land should turn to the Code Napoléon to see exemplified the logical conclusions of the doctrine. "The French law is based upon the application to the landlord and the tenant with the utmost impartiality of the same general propositions; if it gives no undue advantage to the landlord, it certainly does not favour the tenant; it refuses to regard the relation of landlord and tenant as anything exceptional, and applies to their rights and obligations the same principles, and regards them in the same spirit as it would those of the owner and hirer of the most ordinary article; it is the most complete and equitable application of the rules of free trade to the case of the letting and hiring of land."[1] If improvements are made by the tenant without the consent of the landlord (*de mauvaise-foi*), the landlord is entitled to take the improvements at *their original cost*, or require the outgoing tenant to restore the lands to their original condition. But the French law is certainly far superior to that of England and Scotland in this respect:—The tenant may take away anything he can without injury to the subject, and

[1] Richey, *Irish Land Laws*, p. 33.

thus indirectly compel the landlord to give compensation. "The question of improvements is always considered by the French lawyers with the view of deciding whether the tenant should be bound to restore the lands to their original condition."[1] But the French law does not seem well adapted to a progressive state of agriculture, in which the tenant leaves the lands in a better condition than that in which he received them.

It seems necessary, then, to examine, on economic grounds, the principles on which security for tenant's capital, and compensation for improvements, should rest, regard being paid to the interests (real and supposed) of the landlord, the tenant, and the community. It is quite clear that when land is hired for agricultural purposes, some of the capital of the tenant admits of removal without any injury to the subject, and then there seems to be no reason why such removal should not be allowed. But the real difficulty arises when the tenant's capital is inextricably involved in the land, or when it can only be removed with injury to the landlord, or the tenant, or both. With the view of discovering how far the interests of landlord and tenant are identical, and how far opposed, I shall state the opposing claims in the most extreme form in which they are advanced by any considerable section of either class, for if any community of interests is found in the

[1] Richey, p. 28.

extreme sections, *à fortiori* a still greater harmony must exist amongst the more moderate sections. It will be convenient to discuss separately the interests of the public, as the question presents comparatively little difficulty.

1. *The interest (real and supposed) of the landlord.*—(*a*) It is for the interest of the landlord that the tenant should put sufficient capital in the soil for its proper cultivation; (*b*) the landlord wishes to guard against any injury to the land, through the tenant attempting to extract his capital towards the termination of his tenancy, *e.g.* by exhausting cultivation; (*c*) but, apart from injury, he does not wish to have the character of the subject changed, and accordingly claims a veto on any alterations which would have such an effect. A tenant, for example, might increase the letting value of a piece of land by alterations not contemplated when the land was let. In such a case the landlord might object that his proprietary rights had been interfered with, and that no compensation was equitably due. He might argue that he did not wish to sink more capital in the land; that he would have made the alterations himself had he so wished; and that any exceptional increase in value was due to the land in the first place, and only remotely to the tenant. The landlord naturally wishes to retain the power of letting his land for certain definite objects, and is opposed to compensation for capital sunk for other purposes,

however much the letting value may have been increased, and however much capital the tenant may have expended. He maintains that his consent should, first of all, have been obtained. (*d*) The landlord is influenced by the notion that, especially in the case of so-called "permanent" improvements, his consent[1] should be a necessary condition for compensation. The opinion seems to be rapidly gaining ground amongst all classes of landlords that, for the capital which the customary mode of cultivation requires to be sunk in the soil (*e.g.* the ordinary manures, feeding stuffs consumed on the land, etc.), compensation should be made compulsory; and that, even in cases going beyond the usual custom, where anything of value is left in the soil, and when the value will be exhausted in a "limited" time (*e.g.* artificial manures, surface drains, etc.), compensation also might be accorded with advantage. But the landlord conceives his proprietary rights to be endangered if he has to give compensation for any improvement which conveys the idea of permanence if undertaken without his consent. In short, the landlord emphasises what he conceives to be the rights of property.

2. *The interests (real and supposed) of the tenant.*— The tenant, on the other hand, who takes up an extreme position, wishes to get the full value of every-

[1] The Agricultural Holdings Act requires written consent in the case of "permanent" improvements.

thing he may have done. He argues that there is no injury to the landlord, because he demands no more than the increased value due to his efforts. He maintains that the more permanent the improvements or valuable alterations, the more just and necessary it is that he should receive compensation. He regards the character of the subject as of no real importance; he looks on land, so far as affecting the landlord, simply as a rent-producing instrument; and if the rent has been increased by any unusual expenditure of labour and capital, he demands at least a share, and in extreme cases claims the full amount, of the increased letting value. In short, the tenant emphasises the rights of labour.

3. The public at large is interested alike in the rights of property, in the rights of labour, and in cheap and abundant agricultural produce.

It remains then to be seen how far these conflicting interests of landlord and tenant admit of reconciliation, and how the casting vote of the public should be given when the conflict still remains. The question at once resolves itself into two: (1) For what part of the capital he has annexed to the soil shall the tenant be entitled to compensation? (2) By what method should such compensation be calculated and determined?

The first glance shows that there is a *consensus* of opinion on the advisability of compensation in *some* cases; the point at which opinions diverge is where the "improvements" are such as either to change the character of the subject, or are of a permanent nature, whether changing that character or not. There is no doubt that the general principle of compensation must be admitted; the difficulty is, How far is it to be applied? Hitherto, it may be said, the whole controversy seems to have turned on the comparative permanence of the improvements, *e.g.* the distinction is fundamental in the Agricultural Holdings Act. But this *fundamentum divisionis* seems illogical in the extreme. It is probably due to the fact that permanent improvements have been effected in England as a rule, and in Scotland to a considerable extent, by the landlord. The importance attached to "permanence" may also be partly due to the fact that the landlord considers himself to be the best judge[1] of the desirability of permanent improvements, and since they seem to form part and parcel of his land, he conceives it to be both his right and his duty to take the control. He would feel it as a reproof if the tenant undertook an improvement of this kind which was really necessary to the holding, or was at any rate an

[1] "Whilst we are not prepared to recommend the compulsory abolition of all restrictive covenants, we consider that the increased *intelligence* which has been manifested by those engaged in agriculture [presumably tenants], and the general improvement in the system of cultivation which is now in progress, would in many cases justify their removal." —*Report of the Agricultural Commission*, p. 31.

obviously judicious investment of capital. The absurdity, however, of any division made merely on the ground of permanence can be at once seen by an example. Compulsory compensation is proposed for artificial manures left in the soil, but is refused for tile drainage, which alone can make their use advantageous. But the inconsistency can be shown more generally. Permanence is only relative;[1] compensation for an improvement that lasts fifty years is for all practical purposes the same as successive compensation for improvements of a less permanent nature.

The only apparently valid argument in support of the distinction under examination is, that the freedom of action of the landlord is fettered if he has paid for permanent improvements; it may be argued that an improvement for one purpose might be the reverse for another, that the relative importance of different branches of agriculture changes, and that land may be used for other purposes than for agriculture. This argument would have some weight if "permanent" meant literally everlasting, if the purposes for which a piece of land is let were always changing, and, as a matter of fact, improvements effected for one purpose were absolutely useless for any other. But the very reverse is the case; pro-

[1] "Most buildings are good for fifty years, while by the Act (Agricultural Holdings) only thirty are allowed. Most drainage works are good for thirty years, and twenty only are allowed."—*Memorandum on Report by Mr. Clay*, p. 39.

bably no so-called permanent improvement would last much more than fifty years without the further application of labour and capital upon it—even the banks and sluices of the fens require constant repair; and although a certain proportion of land oscillates between a cultivated and an uncultivated state, the proportion is small (and general laws cannot rest on special instances), and although the relative importance of the different branches of agriculture changes, these changes do not constitute a constant succession of revolutions in the cultivation of any particular farm.

The argument, however, suggests a classification of "improvements" founded upon a much more natural and important quality than that of relative permanence. When a landlord lets land for a specific purpose, he has a right to expect that it will not be used for any purpose other than that contemplated; and a tenant taking land for one purpose cannot expect his temporary occupancy to give him the right to use it for something quite different, and to change its character.[1] But what the landlord ought to be prepared to admit, and what the tenant has the right to claim, is that the land shall be let *bona fide* for the purpose contemplated; that the fundamental intention shall not be defeated by the arbitrary restrictive clauses of which

[1] What the law of Scotland calls an "inversion of possession."

nearly every lease furnishes examples. When, therefore, land is let for the purposes of agriculture, or of some specific branch of agriculture, *absolute security should be given for the capital necessary for good husbandry;* but, conversely, the tenant should have *no claim for alterations which really change the character of the subject*, even although these alterations may have added to the letting value. It follows, too, from this distinction, that the landlord should receive compensation for dilapidation and deterioration due to bad husbandry. The principle here laid down has already been admitted in the Ground Game Act, 1880. A landlord cannot now let his land for agricultural purposes and yet at the same time insert a clause forbidding his tenant to kill the vermin which destroy his crops; and it is as absurd to let land for agriculture and forbid drainage (under pain of confiscation at the end of the tenancy), as to let it for agriculture and yet preserve hares and rabbits, —standing water may injure land as much as game.

The distinction here sought to be drawn between (*a*) the use of capital necessary for good husbandry, which, at the same time, does not change the agricultural character of the subject, and (*b*) the use of capital in such a way as to go beyond the general purpose for which the land was let, may easily be made clear by a few examples. As representing the first class, drainage (whether permanent or not), artificial manures, and fences may be taken. It is quite obvious that the character of an agricultural holding cannot be essentially changed by improvements of this order; and while its value may and probably will be increased, it is difficult even to imagine a case in which it might be diminished, and that could be provided for by compensation to the landlord for deterioration. But, in the second class of "improvements" (*b*)—although, it may be observed, *alterations* would be a better designation—the character of the holding is essentially changed. If, for example, a tenant breaks up permanent pasture, as was very commonly done at the commencement of the century owing to the high price of corn; or if he brings moorland under the plough; or if he turns his farm into a rabbit warren; in all these cases a radical change is made in the character of the subject. Although it is possible that in every instance named the letting value of the holding might be increased, it is quite clear that the claim for compulsory compensation rests on quite a different footing in the case of capital necessary for good husbandry and capital speculatively used in radical alterations. Whether anything whatever which increases the letting value, which seems to be the popular definition of an improvement, should receive compulsory compensation will be discussed in the next chapter; but, in the first place, an enumeration of the requisites of good husbandry must be attempted, and the modifications introduced by the condition that they do not change the character of the subject must be taken into account. The attempt must be regarded as an illustration of the distinction on which it is thought legislation should be based, and not as furnishing a list of requisites which admits neither of extension, contraction, nor modification.

Although the division of "improvements" into permanent and non-permanent cannot be accepted as a basis for compensation or non-compensation, the distinction points to other characteristics of importance. As a rule, for example, the permanent improvements are such as can be made by the landlord if he chooses, whilst the more temporary improvements, *e.g.* the judicious use of artificial manures, must in general be done by the farmer. Again, the methods of valuation, as will be seen later, do not present exactly the same kind of difficulty. I shall accordingly just enumerate the requisites of good husbandry which are of a relatively permanent nature, and shall endeavour to show that any improvement made by the tenant in this direction will not eventually change the character of the holding.

The following are some of the most important improvements of a "permanent" nature which may be considered as necessary for good husbandry: thorough drainage of the land in cultivation; drainage of grass lands, so far as necessary; suitable accommodation for labourers and shepherds required on the farm; suitable house and yard accommodation for cattle; subdivision of farm into necessary enclosures; taking out boulders from land in cultivation; construction of roads necessary for working the farm. It will, I think, be granted that an improvement in any of these particulars does not go beyond the rules of good husbandry, and a little reflection will show that the character of the holding is not changed. Under-drains cannot even affect the nature of the surface, though they increase its efficiency—draining a field is not like draining a loch. Again, to dig up boulders in cultivated land, so as to be able to plough deeper, is very different from reclaiming moorland. Buildings and fences can, if considered injurious (though the case is hardly conceivable), be removed, and the land be brought to the *status quo ante.* The case of roads, which are very expensive to construct, shows that a tenant would not be over-hasty in embarking on any improvements which he did not consider necessary or likely to be beneficial. If, then, in any of these particulars the tenant has improved the condition of the holding without changing (except in value) its agricultural character, his claim for compensation seems incontestable. By whom and on what principles the compensation should be determined will be discussed later.

In the second class of improvements according to the rules of good husbandry, which are of a comparatively temporary nature, popular attention has been principally directed to the outlays of the tenant on manures and feeding-stuffs consumed on the land. Here the equity of compensation for whatever portion is unexhausted on the termination of the tenancy has been generally admitted, and the only difficulty lies in the proper method of calculating the value. But there is another kind of improvement of at least equal importance, although not capable of such easy definition. A tenant's energy, skill, and industry may improve the fertility of the land, just as much as the actual addition of plant-producing ingredients to the soil; indeed, the latter operation is useless unless coupled with the former. Slovenly and unskilful cultivation may easily neutralise the advantages of an abundant use of artificial manures. Thorough cultivation, cleanness, and condition of the soil, ought to be considered, and would, in fact, be considered by any one taking a farm, just as much as the natural qualities and the artificial elements which have been superadded. Land cannot be kept in high condition without the expenditure of capital in many ways. It seems reasonable, then, that increased general fertility should be considered a proper subject for compensation to the tenant, and, conversely, decreased value should be made good to the landlord.

The question remains: By what method should the compensation be calculated and determined? and this again may be divided into two questions:—

(1.) Who shall decide the amount of the compensation?

(2.) By what principles shall they be governed in their decision?

(1.) As regards the valuators, the natural presumption is, as always, against Government interference, if it can be avoided; and it seems desirable that, at any rate in the first place, arbiters should be chosen by the parties, and they again should choose their own oversman. This is the method generally adopted in Scotland in the transfer of stock by the outgoing tenant to the landlord, where the pecuniary interests at stake are larger than would be the case in the valuation of improvements. No doubt, occasionally, difficulties have occurred, but on the whole, the system has worked satisfactorily. There seems to be no more reason for the appointment of official valuators for the estimation of unexhausted improvements than for the valuation of stock. At present, if a landlord thinks the outgoing tenant has left the land in a better condition, he demands a higher rent, and the incoming tenant has to form his own opinion whether he shall accede to the demand or not. The mere fact of a share of the value of the improved condition going to the outgoing tenant can make no difference whatever to the incomer, and the division of the increased value seems a proper subject for arbitration. At any rate in this, as in all other industrial matters, it seems absurd to resort to Government before the voluntary system of selection has even been tried. The Commissioners think it advisable[1] "to have in each county a certain number of thoroughly qualified men, named by the Sheriff-Principal, one or other of whom shall be appointed by the Sheriff or his Substitute to act as oversman in the case of the arbiters, appointed by the parties, failing to agree upon the selection of an oversman, or as sole arbiter, should there be any failure in the nomination of arbiter by the parties;" but it will be time enough to think of the remedy when the necessity for it has been proved. Of course the fees, expenses, etc., connected with the arbitration, are to be paid by the parties interested. It is hardly likely that the country or the county would submit to taxation for the purpose; but if the system is to be self-supporting, and the official valuators are to subsist on their fees, it seems probable either that the fees would prove prohibitive or the officials incompetent.

(2.) There can be no doubt as to the general principle of calculating compensation, unless agricultural values are supposed to follow a law different from all others. Whether an improvement will be made or not depends, no doubt, on a comparison of the probable cost with the probable profits, but when once the thing has been done, cost has nothing to do with its value. And the Commissioners have

[1] Report, etc., p. 31.

acted wisely in recommending an amendment of the provisions of the Agricultural Holdings Act (the principles of which, they think, should be made compulsory in all cases where such compensation is not otherwise provided for), so as "to make the compensation depend upon the additional value of the holding." The dangers of any other method may be illustrated by a reference to the case of artificial manures, although, at first sight, it seems plausible to calculate the quantity of manure applied, and the period of its probable efficiency. (1) There would always be a danger of collusion between the merchants and the tenant. (2) The manures might have been applied, but owing to bad or slovenly cultivation, or to impoverishing crops (*e.g.* potatoes), the value of the soil may not have been increased, and yet the tenant may have a large claim for compensation. (3) The tenant might have applied manures bearing compensation, and yet by mixing with them certain ingredients (*e.g.* some form of dissolvent) have converted them into stimulating manures, and have added nothing to the value of the holding. (4) From the nature of the case the claim for compensation, reckoned in the manner proposed, could only be made for the expenditure of the last two or three years; and in the earlier years the tenant might have had much greater expenses in bringing the land into good condition, for which, however, he would receive no compensation. The general principle that value and not cost must be considered applies to both temporary and permanent improvements; but of course in both cases it would be quite open to the arbiters to take into consideration the cost, etc., as part of the evidence on which to found their judgment. In the same way, as Lord Vernon suggests,[1] the crops to which manures have been applied might be taken as evidence of their value, though this alone does not appear to be sufficient, nor does the limitation to this kind of evidence appear necessary. Practical men, for example, compare the growth of plants on the bits of waste that are scattered over every farm with the growth on the cultivated portions; they profess to be able to judge of the condition of ploughed land by the tread of the foot, and there is a proverb that a blind man can tell good land by the size of the thistles and docks. It is quite evident that in judging of general fertility, as in judging of stock, numberless minute considerations would influence the arbiters, and for practical purposes it would be the height of presumption for any legislator to give precise instructions for valuation. To deny that general fertility can be valued is to deny what is every day taking place.

It may, however, be objected that it would be impossible to determine how much of this fertility and good condition was due to the action of any

[1] Report, p. 35.

tenant, as there might be different arbiters at the commencement and at the termination of the tenancy. But this objection is not so forcible as at first sight appears. Many facts could be placed on record at the commencement of the tenancy, and the condition of the land could be fairly described; and the average produce at the two periods compared with other farms in the district would, allowances being made for other causes of variation, form a basis for calculation. Theoretically it would be possible to adopt a system according to which the condition of land could at different periods be described as so much above or below par, and allowances be made accordingly, just as school inspectors have certain standards for reading, writing, etc.; and no one would deny that the progress of a school in these respects, due to a change of teachers, could be fairly estimated, although the inspectors were different. At any rate, if the principle were admitted in law, there is no doubt that it could be carried into practice; and the calculations, though necessarily rough at first, would become more and more accurate, as the different parties concerned became familiar with this kind of arbitration.

One other difficulty remains to be noticed: How much of the increased value is to go to the tenant? Is he to obtain the whole increase in value estimated as due to the improvement, or only a portion? It is often argued (*e.g.* by the Duke of Argyll)[1] that the former alternative would be unjust to the landlord. In under-drainage, for example, the tenant might expend (the figures are only taken for illustration) £6 per acre on land worth £30 per acre (*i.e.* with a rental of £1); and the improvement might be valued at £10, that is, as increasing the value of the rental by one-third (6s. 8d.) In such a case, if the tenant were to leave the farm at once, and were to receive the full increase of £10, the owner might justly argue that he was unfairly treated; the tenant's drainage-pipes, labour, etc., would have produced nothing unless applied to land furnished to him by the landowner in a certain condition (*i.e.* in need of drainage); in fact, taking the capital requisite to make the improvement, furnished by landlord and tenant respectively, the former is, in the example taken, five times the latter; and after making all due allowance for "wages of superintendence" and exceptional skill, still it would seem equitable that at any rate a share of the profit should go to the landlord. But the difficulty may be avoided practically by a very simple method. It was pointed out as a characteristic of permanent improvements that they could be effected by the landlord if he chose to do so, and hitherto that has been to a great

[1] *Commercial Principles applied to Contracts for the Hire of Land.*

extent the case. All then that equity seems to demand is that the landlord should always have the option of effecting the improvements himself, the tenant paying a certain percentage (say five per cent.) on the capital expended, this percentage being in fact an addition to the rent on account of the greater efficiency of the instrument (land). But if the landlord refused to undertake the work, and the tenant took the whole risk of making improvements, which the arbiters at the termination of the tenancy might or might not think of value, then it seems only just that the whole advantage (if any) should accrue to the tenant, it being always understood that the character of the subject is not changed. It is very improbable that the tenant would, with the chances of an unfavourable valuation before his eyes, enter on any improvement which did not promise to give a good return—a prudent tenant, indeed, would always require a good margin; and probably the practice of the future would not differ so much from that of the present as is generally supposed or feared, for wherever any margin seemed likely to accrue the landlord would wish to forestall the tenant. If, however, the landowner argues that he might wish to defer this investment of capital, he has always the option of not letting the land at all; but if he does let the land, the casting vote of the public is on the side of the tenant—the nation at large has certainly no interest in deferring the period of most efficient cultivation of its land.

The general effect, if the proposals suggested in this chapter were carried out, would no doubt be in the first place to cause a rise in rent; just as at present a farmer will pay more rent to a good than to a bad landlord, so, if security for capital were given, tenants in general could afford to pay more rent. Hence it follows, as the Duke of Argyll has pointed out, that compensation for improvements would not benefit the tenant so much as he anticipates, because the privilege itself would have a pecuniary value. But indirectly the tenant would gain, for he would be able to employ more capital and obtain greater gross profits; for, as was shown in the examination of the theory of rent, the interest of the landlord in the tenant's applications of capital to land ceases at the point at which they do not yield rent. The good tenant would also gain in security of tenure, for the landlord would not evict if he expected a heavy bill for compensation; on the other hand, the bad farmer would be stimulated by the fear of having to pay for deterioration, and if he did deteriorate the land, it is not for the public interest that fixity of tenure should in his case be considerable; in fact, giving the landlord compensation for deterioration would tend greatly to improve farming. The gain to the public is obvious: any improvement in the most important of all industries would at once be reflected to manufactures and trade; and indirectly in the way described by Adam Smith,[1] the political strength, the stability of the national wealth, and the commercial supremacy of the country would be placed on a firmer basis.

[1] *Cf.* Chap. I.

CHAPTER XI.

THE RIGHTS OF PROPERTY AND THE RIGHTS OF LABOUR.

"It is ordained, for the safetie and favour of puir people that labouris the ground, that they and all utheris that hes taken or sall take landes in time to come fra lordes, and hes termes and zeires thereof, that suppose the lordes sell or annaly that land or landes, the takers sall remaine with their tackes unto the ischew of their termes quhais handes that ever they landes cum to, for siklike maill as they took them for."—*Statute of* 1449.

"Etwas muss er sein eigen nennen
Oder der Mensch wird morden und brennen."
SCHILLER.

THERE is no doubt that a considerable section of the occupiers of land in Great Britain think legislation should be carried much further than was suggested in the last chapter. The arguments principally used may be reduced to three: 1st, That every man has a right to the fruits of his own labour, and that this, and this alone, constitutes the fundamental justification of private property; 2d, That no injustice is done to the landlord if compensation is only given when the letting value has been increased by the capital and labour of the occupier (in whatever manner applied); 3d, That the community is benefited by anything which increases the gross agricultural produce.

The first proposition, which makes labour the basis of property, is supported by three of the greatest English philosophers—John Locke, Adam Smith, and John Stuart Mill. In Locke we find the proposition generally joined with two others, which have, however, a similar origin: (1) That the right of acquisition must be limited—"if one exceeds the bounds of moderation and takes more than he has need of, he undoubtedly takes what belongs to others;" (2) "Every one ought to have as much property as is necessary for his support." The following passage may be taken as a fair summary of Locke's views: "The measure of property Nature has well set by the extent of man's labour and the conveniences of life; no man's labour could subdue or appropriate all, nor could his enjoyment consume more than a small part; so that it was impossible for any man, this way, to intromit upon the right of another, or acquire to himself a property to the prejudice of his neighbour, who would still have room for as good and as large a possession. This measure, we see, confines every man's possession to a very moderate proportion, and such as he might appropriate to himself, without injury to anybody." Many passages might be quoted from *The Wealth of Nations* to show that the views of Locke were held by Adam Smith. As examples, the following may be taken: "Labour was the first price, the original purchase-money that was paid for all things." "The property which every man has in his own labour, as it is the original foundation of all other property, so it is the most sacred and inviolable. The patrimony of a poor man lies in the strength and the dexterity of his hands; and to hinder him from employing this strength and dexterity in any manner he thinks proper without injury to his neighbour, is a plain violation of the most sacred property." But the opinions of Locke and Adam Smith mainly influence the present generation through the expression they find in Mill. Mill commences his analysis of property (*Principles of Political Economy*, bk. ii. chs. i. ii.), by saying that the foundation of the whole institution is the right of producers to what they have themselves produced. Applying this fundamental conception to land, he argues that "if the land derived its productive power wholly from Nature and not at all from industry, or if there were any means of discriminating what is derived from each source, it not only would not be necessary, but it would be the height of injustice, to let the gift of Nature be engrossed by individuals."[1] He then, however, goes on to maintain that though land is not the produce of industry, most of its valuable

[1] Bk. ii. ch. ii. sect. 5.

qualities are; that labour is required, not only for using but for fashioning the instrument: and concludes by asserting, with all the recklessness of a logician, that "whenever, in any country, the proprietor, generally speaking, ceases to be the improver, political economy has nothing to say in defence of landed property as there established. In no sound theory of private property was it ever contemplated that the proprietor of land should be merely a sinecurist quartered on it."[1] The danger of making startling political statements guarded by a number of qualifications, lies in the fact that it is always inconvenient to quote a qualified dictum, and as celebrated writers are much oftener quoted than read, the context soon disappears altogether. At the very outset, however, Mill supplements the labour theory of property by three important additions: (1) Any person has the right to receive by gift or fair agreement (*i.e.* without force or fraud) the products of the labour of others; (2) Capital is the result of labour, and the present owners have obtained it from the original producers by gift or fair contract; (3) A title, after a certain period, must be given by prescription. The last proposition is of the greatest importance, and is strongly enforced. "Possession which has not been legally questioned within a moderate number of years ought to be, as by the laws of all nations it is, a complete

[1] *Principles of Political Economy*, bk. ii. ch. ii. sect. 6.

title." The doctrine of full compensation in case of expropriation follows immediately, and is most emphatically stated. "It is due to landowners and to owners of any property whatever, recognised as such by the state, that they shall not be dispossessed of it without receiving its pecuniary value, or an annual income equal to what they derived from it. This is due on the general principles on which property rests. If the land was bought with the produce of the labour and abstinence of themselves or their ancestors, compensation is due to them on that ground; even if otherwise, it is still due on the ground of prescription. . . . When the property is of a kind to which peculiar affections attach themselves, the compensation ought to exceed a bare pecuniary equivalent [*pretium affectionis*]. But subject to this proviso, the State is at liberty to deal with landed property as the general interests of the community may require, even to the extent, if it so happen, of doing with the whole what is done with a part, whenever a bill is passed for a railroad or a new street."[1] In effect the doctrine of Mill amounts to this—that the landlords have not an indefeasible right to the land, but they have such a right to the full value of the land; and at another place he says this value should include the value of all future expectations.

It may then be considered as a maxim of English

[1] Mill's *Prin. Polit. Econ.*, bk. ii. ch. ii. sect. 6.

political economy that if the landlord is deprived of any proprietary right full compensation should be given, and the question of giving further privileges to the occupiers of land by legislation resolves itself into a question of expense and expediency. The basis of the compensation proposed to be given in the last chapter to tenants for their improvements is that, so long as the character of the holding is not changed, there is no infringement of proprietary rights: all the landlord is bound to do, when he chooses to let his land for agriculture, is to furnish it, or allow the tenant to furnish it, with the requisites of good husbandry under a progressive system of agriculture. But many people argue that whether the character of the holding is changed by the tenant or not, if only the letting value has been increased, the tenant has the right to full or partial compensation, and that there is here also no infringement of proprietary rights, and no compensation to the landlord due from the public. That the tenant should equitably obtain the full increase on the letting value can only be maintained if the ground on which he operates is absolutely valueless, which is manifestly absurd, as the possibility of improvement has itself a market value. But I should be inclined to go further, and say that the temporary occupier has no equitable claim for compensation for "alterations" undertaken without the consent of the landlord, unless the State gives to the landlord due compensation for depriving him of the right to let his land for whatever purpose he pleases. The contrary proposition is maintained, especially in favour of crofters who reclaim land, and then have to pay rent on the full value of their own improvements. And no doubt the common sense of justice is rudely shocked when such cases occur, for, as a rule, the reclaimer is the best of peasants, whilst the rack-renter is the worst of landlords; and when the landlord is an absentee, and all the deepest feelings of the tenant are bound up with his little holding, the privileges of the landlord and the burdens of the tenant seem altogether disproportioned to their services in the economic system, and an agitation is raised for a new definition of the rights of the lords of the soil. But although it be granted that for every wrong the law should provide a remedy, the remedy may consist in exceptional legislation for an exceptional case. It may, for example, be expedient to fix the hours of labour in some employments, and yet in general to leave the question to the contracting parties, and, without multiplying examples, it may be said that the whole of the factory legislation consists of a series of regulations qualifying in particular instances the general principle of freedom of contract. And in the same way it is quite possible to pass exceptional measures for exceptional cases in the hire of land without altogether changing the content of the present conception of private property in land, which would be the case if a tenant is to be allowed to make radical alterations on the subject, and claim compensation for them against the express command of the owner of the land. But it might be made incumbent on the landlord to expressly warn the crofter not to enter on reclamation. If the tenant persisted, the landlord might evict, but if without eviction he allowed the reclamation to proceed, he should be considered to have given his consent, and be liable to make full compensation for their value. A landlord or his agent ought to know what is being done with the land; but, at any rate a tenant might give notice, and, unless threatened with eviction in case of proceeding, make his improvements *de bonne foi*, and be entitled to their value. And there seems to be little objection to going even somewhat further in the case of very small holdings. Crofters cannot be expected to have any very accurate notions of the actual positive law, and their conduct is for the most part guided by traditions and customs. There can be no doubt, too, that whenever courts and lawyers have substituted written law for flexible custom, the poor have suffered by the change, and in interpreting a contract for the hire of land, regard should be paid to the natural expectations of the small tenant as well as to the strict rights of the large landlord. "When called in to determine the legal powers of the chieftain over the domains which gave sustenance to the clan, Scottish jurisprudence had long since passed the point at which it could take notice of the vague limitations on completeness of dominion imposed by the claims of the clansmen, and it was inevitable that it should convert the patrimony of many into the estate of one."[1] It appears then equitable in the case of the Highland crofters to reverse the presumption of the law, and to give the tenant the full benefit of any improvements (radical alterations or not) which are not expressly and distinctly forbidden by the landlord under pain of eviction.

But many of the friends of the crofters would go much further. In the interests of maximum gross produce and a large increase in the rural population, they would compel the large proprietors to let a considerable part of their estates in small holdings. In this proposal I think few economists would concur. I do not imagine the gross produce would be very much increased, if, indeed, there was not a falling off, and the net produce which could be sent to the towns would almost certainly be less. However much the large sheep-farms were subdivided, they could not well be made to carry more sheep, whilst they would require more labour. No doubt the rural population might be artificially kept up; but the case of the Scottish Highlands is not peculiar—the rural population all over Europe (even in

[1] Maine's *Ancient Law*, p. 238.

the countries of peasant proprietors) is steadily declining. The causes of the decrease are obvious. In the first place, nearly every improvement in agriculture admits of a diminution of the number of labourers: and secondly, the attractions of the towns and the higher rates of wages make the country people themselves willing to change their employment. Poets no doubt will always declaim against their infatuation—

> "O fortunatos nimium sua si bona norint
> Agricolas!"—

but husbandmen, like other people, are greatly influenced by the prospects of material comfort. And it is only by constant immigration to the towns, and coming into the sphere of industrial competition, that the standard of comfort of the rural population can be raised. If no check is placed on the mobility of labour, the wages and advantages of any occupation tend to become proportioned to the skill and effort involved, and there can be no doubt that, if competition is allowed free play, the wages of those engaged in agriculture must rank relatively much higher than at present. When this rise takes place it will be for the economic advantage of proprietors to induce the rural population to remain by making concessions. But any attempt to increase artificially the proportion of rural to town population will inevitably tend to lower the "standard of comfort" of the former, and to make their labour inefficient.

In the meantime the force of public opinion is very powerful to prevent injustice, and its power must not be disregarded because it is not sharply defined. The rights that rest only on sentiment are better enforced by the expression of impartial public opinion than by the learned judgments of the Bench. It is worth observing that towards the end of the sixteenth century precisely the same outcry was raised in England against the establishment of extensive sheep-walks, and the complaints of W. S., in his "*Brief conceipte touching the Commonwealth of England*,[1] are as bitter as those of Professor Blackie. "Those sheepe is the cause of all this mischieves, for they have driven husbandry out of the country by the which was increased before all kindes of victailles and now altogether sheepe, sheepe, sheepe." But the agriculture of England was not ruined, nor the natural increase of the power and wealth of the people prevented, and the increase of sheep then as now was due to economic causes, which it would have been useless or harmful to counteract by the strong hand of the law.

[1] Published 1588.

CHAPTER XII.

ON THE PROBABLE APPRECIATION OF GOLD, AND CYCLES OF INFLATION AND DEPRESSION OF TRADE.

"Given the fertility of the mines, and the total quantity of money in circulation, prices in the aggregate must be lower through the world, as a whole, in proportion to the general industry and skill of mankind, and the extent and facility of their trade."—T. E. Cliffe Leslie.

It was recently stated in the House of Commons by Mr. Goschen, one of the highest authorities on the subject, that a continuous appreciation of gold seemed probable, and that the appreciation had already begun. The fact has an important bearing on the question of leases, and indirectly on other matters of the greatest interest to all connected with land. As the subject has hitherto been only discussed by specialists, and, as far as I have observed, has not been alluded to by the multitude of writers and speakers on the land question, it seems to fall naturally within the scope of the present work to examine the reasons why an appreciation of gold may be anticipated, and to deduce some of the more practical results. An appreciation of gold is, of course, the same thing as a general fall in prices, the very meaning of the expression is that a given amount of gold purchases more commodities than before. But general prices depend on a variety of causes, some operating in the same direction, and others antagonistic. There is no proposition better established in Political Economy than that, under certain conditions, the value of money (by which is meant not the rate of interest, but a high or low level of prices of things in general) varies inversely as its quantity multiplied by the rapidity of circulation. But the conditions laid down are, for practical purposes, of the highest moment. The two elements in the law—the quantity of money and the rapidity of circulation—may be taken separately. It is easy to see, under the assumptions to be indicated, that the more money there is the less will be the exchange value of every piece. The necessary assumptions are—(1) that the quantity of commodities to be exchanged, and the number of exchanges to be effected, remain the same; (2) that money is used only for purposes of currency;—that is, that no account is taken of the other uses to which the material of which it is made can be applied; (3) that money passes from hand to hand at every transaction—credit, and even barter, being non-existent. Under these conditions it is obvious that the value of money must vary inversely as its quantity; if the quantity is doubled, general prices will be doubled; if the quantity is diminished by one-half, general prices will fall one-half. The best practical application of the law is furnished by the issue of inconvertible paper notes. In this case it is easily shown theoretically, that the conditions indicated being realised to the same degree, the value of the paper rises and falls inversely as the quantity, and every issue of such notes has proved to demonstration the truth of the theory. The financiers of the French Revolution imagined that, if their *assignats* and *mandats* represented land, no depreciation could take place, but in spite of the most severe penalties a depreciation ensued, which reduced the value of the notes practically to zero. The Directors of the Bank of England imagined, during the period of the restriction of gold payments, that if they only issued their notes on the usual securities, and at the usual rate of interest, depreciation would be impossible; so convinced were they, indeed, that when the depreciation occurred, they denied the palpable fact, and maintained that notes were not depreciated, but that gold was appreciated.

As regards the other element in the law—"the rapidity of circulation"—it must be pointed out, in the first place, that the phrase is inaccurate and misleading. The expression, suggested by Mill—the efficiency of money—is much more appropriate. A little reflection will show that the same effect must be produced on general prices, if one piece of money is used twice, or two pieces of money are used once in effecting any amount of transactions, and this is all that is implied by rapidity of circulation. Any increase in the use of the money in existence is equivalent, in its effects, to an increase in its quantity.

It follows from these general considerations that—

(1.) The first cause to be taken into account in investigating any change in the value of money is the increase or decrease in the quantity. Every one knows that the discoveries of mines in the sixteenth century caused a general rise in prices, and that the discoveries in Australia and California thirty years ago caused a fall in the value of gold. Now there is no doubt that the production of gold has been steadily declining. Taking periods of five years, the total production in the world has been estimated as follows:—

1857–1861, ...	£139,684,000.
1862–1866, ...	136,343,000.
1867–1871, ...	133,218,000.
1872–1876, ...	118,069,000.
1877–1881, ...	114,872,000.[1]

The production of 1882 is given at £21,777,000, which, it will be observed, is below the average of the last quinquennial period. So far, then, as the quantity of gold is concerned, a rise in its value, or a general fall of prices, may be expected.

[1] *New York Financial Review*, p. 25.

(2.) The next important consideration is the amount of transactions which have to be effected by the gold. Here it is necessary to get rid of a prevailing misconception. Many people have a hazy notion that the substitutes for gold can be indefinitely increased, and that the quantity of the actual metal is, in the modern world, of small importance. The error has been admirably exposed by Mr. Giffen in his work on *Stock Exchange Securities*, and in an essay on the *Depreciation of Gold since* 1848.[1] He shows that the whole superstructure of credit must rest on a gold basis; even in the wildest speculative mania on the Stock Exchange, a limit to the rise of prices is set by the amount of gold on which it ultimately rests. It may be true that 99½ per cent. of the commercial transactions of this country are effected without the use of the precious metals, but the ½ per cent. of gold required is absolutely indispensable. It may be that if all claims on all the banks were presented at once not fourpence in the pound would be forthcoming, but the whole banking system rests upon that fourpence. Whatever economies in the use of gold are made, gold is required for three purposes in every country with a gold currency—

(1.) To form the ultimate banking reserve;

(2.) To meet foreign drain;

(3.) For certain currency purposes.

It is upon this third function of gold that Mr. Giffen

[1] Essay II. in *Essays on Finance.*

founds his method for calculating appreciation or depreciation.

"Other things being the same, it follows from a general rise of prices that a greater quantity of metal must be employed in circulation to do the same work as before. If other commodities are unchanged, and population and business are the same, then if a sovereign is reduced to the value of half a sovereign, double the number of sovereigns will be required to make the same payments. Any similar reduction of value must be accompanied by a similar increase of quantity. No doubt the qualification that other things must be the same is very important; but it appears to be not altogether impossible to ascertain whether the requirements of a community for a gold circulation in proportion to the population have or have not changed, so that if they have not we should be able to affirm that a general rise in prices must have involved an addition to the circulation disproportionate to the increase of population and of trade."[1]

Now, when we apply these principles we find further reasons for anticipating continuous appreciation. The population and commerce of the gold-using countries are developing at a very rapid rate, and the number of the gold-using countries has of late years been steadily increasing. It follows, then, that the demands for the "small change" of gold coins must

[1] Giffen's *Essays on Finance*, p. 84.

also steadily increase. The remark applies especially to America and our Colonies. For the last five years America has on balance been importing and not exporting gold.[1]

	Exports.	Imports.	Net Imports.
1878, . .	£9,204,455	£13,330,215	£4,125,760
1879, . .	4,587,614	5,624,948	1,037,334
1880, . .	3,639,025	80,758,396	77,119,371
1881, . .	2,565,132	101,031,259	98,466,127
1882, . .	32,587,880	34,377,054	1,789,176

The exportation from Australia has also been steadily decreasing.[2]

1866— £9,618,442	1871—£7,605,898	1876—£5,793,374
1867— £8,783,489	1872—£7,597,021	1877—£7,295,868
1868— £9,351,191	1873—£9,367,130	1878—£5,567,084
1869—£10,382,955	1874—£7,662,925	1879—£2,403,302
1870— £8,237,367	1875—£6,949,516	1880—£4,171,749

It must be remembered, too, that more than half of the total production of gold in the world is in America and Australia, whilst the condition of Russia, the only other country that has a similar production, is so peculiar financially and politically that its exports of gold are very spasmodic. Another fact must be noticed in reference to America. The people have increased their holdings of gold to the extent of about forty millions of dollars during the past year, and decreased their holdings of silver two millions, whilst the amount of bank-notes and legal

[1] *New York Financial Review*, p. 25.

[2] *Ibid.*, p. 24.

tenders has diminished nearly nineteen millions. The explanation may be partly found, no doubt, in recent legislation making it compulsory on the banks to hold a certain proportion of silver, which makes people wish to hoard gold, but the principal reason is to be found in the fact that in new-settled and undeveloped districts gold is preferred to paper.

(3.) Another cause which does not lie so much on the surface is operating in the same direction as the increase of commerce and population. With every improvement in the means of communication the area of customary prices is diminished; prices in the same country tend to reach the same level, and even prices in different countries exhibit the same tendency. In the sixteenth century the discoveries of the precious metals only acted for a considerable time along the established lines of commerce; there were enormous differences in prices in the same country. In modern times it has often been pointed out that the introduction of a railway at once raises prices. It may be taken as an established fact that places where money is abundant and commerce active have a higher level of prices than is to be found in remote places. But this general levelling of prices must be a levelling down and not a levelling up. The more that remote places are brought under central influences the more "small change" will they require. The same quantity of money cannot effect the exchanges at a high level of prices which were formerly effected at a lower level, and, besides, the number of exchanges also increases.

An appeal to actual prices confirms the view that a general fall is taking place.[1] In general a revival in trade is characterised by a rise in prices of commodities; but in the present revival, although the volume of trade has increased and orders have vastly improved, prices still rule low. It is true the prices of sheep and cattle are high, but this is owing to exceptional causes, and it is very improbable that this high range of prices will be maintained.

There is another characteristic of general prices which should be considered in reference to leases. There can be no doubt that periods of inflation and depression tend to come in cycles of about ten years. The economic history of the last hundred years shows the fact, and it is easy to see theoretically that oscillations between inflations and depressions are to be expected. Supply can never continue for a long period precisely adjusted to demand, and credit is sure to be overstrained after a short period of prosperity; but a change in credit operates on prices as effectually as a change in the quantity of money, and a small excess in supply is apt to produce a more than proportionate fall in price. It follows, then, that the rent offered or demanded in a lease should be calculated in respect to these cyclical

[1] Cf. *Economist Commercial History and Review of* 1882. February 24, 1883.

changes. There can be no doubt that most of the farms taken about ten years ago were taken at too high a rent, whilst at present perhaps the landlord is at a disadvantage if he still elects to abide by leases, unless the appreciation of gold should operate more on prices than the revival of trade.

CHAPTER XIII.

CONCLUSION.

"Der Worte sind genug gewechselt;
Lasst mich auch endlich Thaten sehn."—GOETHE.

IN the foregoing chapters I have been careful to indicate the various exceptions to the general propositions on which the argument rests, for there is no doubt that the extreme and intolerant form in which economic principles are often applied to practice, and the dogmatism on the supposed necessary harmony of the interests of all classes under all conceivable circumstances, have tended to destroy the legitimate influence of political economy. If a general rule is applied with too much rigour, by a necessary reaction the exception is insisted on with too much force; and since a concrete exception is always more clearly seen than an abstract proposition, the principle is often lost sight of altogether. But, on the other hand, the attempt to introduce in a judicial manner a number of qualifications and saving clauses tends to obscure the real points at issue and to create uncertainty where no reasonable doubt ought to remain. I propose then, in conclusion, to disregard the appearance of dogmatism, and to state briefly the main conclusions suggested by this inquiry.

In the first place the progress of civilisation continually imposes new functions upon Government, but since the capacity of the individual members who constitute a Government does not increase with the same rapidity, the assumption of new functions should only take place when urgent necessity is proved, and relief should be sought in the abandonment of functions of relatively less importance. Accordingly the presumption in favour of *laisser faire*, as the history of progressive societies clearly proves, tends to become stronger and not weaker as people dazzled by the success of some new form of governmental interference are inclined to imagine. The control of Government is necessarily a control of routine; Government cannot even collect its taxes on industry without imposing vexatious and harassing restrictions which hinder its natural development, and any intervention between the parties to an industrial contract checks still more effectually that tendency to variation which is the root of all progress. The result obtained from an actual conflict of interests is in general more beneficial to the society than a result due to an authoritative decree issued by a fallible Government according to what at the time appear to be the equities of the case. In matters of business self-interest is the supreme motive-power, and this self-interest produces energy, readiness, and self-reliance. The survivor in an industrial conflict is in general the fittest to survive.

It follows as a corollary from the general presumption in favour of *laisser faire*, that laws which are no longer adapted to the changed condition of society should be abolished as speedily as possible. An antiquated statute can often be used as an instrument of injustice, and thus tends to bring the whole law of the realm into disrepute. There are many anomalies in the present laws affecting the ownership of land, and in the popular imagination they taint the whole system; results which are mainly due to economic causes are attributed to preferential laws, and a feeling of class hostility is aroused and perpetuated. People are induced to abandon the safe guidance of well-established *media axiomata*, or common-sense maxims, as the phrase may be translated in this connection, and to apply first principles, which present a delusive appearance of simplicity, to the concrete difficulties with which private property in land must, under nearly all circumstances, be involved. They discover, in the same way as the two young gentlemen in the time of Swift discovered that there is no God, that land is not thc result of labour, that labour is the only equitable basis of private property, and that the Golden Age can be brought back to the weary world by the nationalisation of the land. The success which has attended Mr. George's *Progress and Poverty* in this country is significant, and it is no sufficient answer to a work of that kind to show that theoretically it rests upon a complete misapprehension and perversion of economic doctrine, and that practically the proposals which it advocates would do nothing towards effecting the end in view. The success of this work, of which a simple analysis forms an obvious and severe condemnation, points to the fact that private property in land creates a strong though ill-defined sense of injustice in the mass of society, and the sentiment is to be largely attributed to the doubtful privileges accorded by the law to a particular class. The abolition of the laws which give rise to the abuses of nominal ownership, and prevent the simple transfer of landed property, would at the same time allay the popular discontent and place the present system of ownership on a firmer basis. The landowning class would be strengthened by the elimination of useless members, and by giving the hand of fellowship to the peasant proprietor on one side and to the merchant on the other. And in doing this they would only follow out a constitutional tradition.

"The great peculiarity," says Stubbs,[1] "of the baronial estate in England as compared with the Continent is the absence of the idea of caste; the English lords do not answer to the nobles of France or to the princes and counts of Germany, because in our system the theory of nobility of blood as conveying political privilege has no legal recognition. English nobility is merely the nobility of the hereditary counsellors of the Crown, the right to give counsel being involved at one time in the tenure of land, at another in the fact of summons, at another in the terms of a patent; it is the result rather than the cause of peerage. . . . Such legal nobility does not of course preclude the existence of real nobility, socially privileged and defined by ancient purity of descent, or even by connection with the legal nobility of the peerage; but the English law does not regard the man of most ancient and purest descent as entitled thereby to any right or privilege which is not shared by every freeman." But the remnants of the laws of primogeniture and entail appear to confer peculiar privileges on landowners, and the idea strongly prevails that the English aristocracy is kept in possession of the national land simply by these survivals of feudal law. Accordingly the position of the "real nobility" would be improved by the abandonment of laws which only

[1] *Constitutional History*, vol. ii. ch. xv. p. 176.

serve to create popular irritation and to make work for the legal profession. It is extremely improbable that the simplest system of transfer possible would make any considerable difference in the size of estates or in the class of owners, but it would make a considerable difference in the way in which large estates and noble owners are regarded by the rest of the community.

But as regards the hire of land, something more than the mere abolition of preferential or antiquated laws seems to be necessary, whether we consider large or small occupiers, though the grounds of Government interference are somewhat different in the two cases. In a summary of the argument it is convenient to notice the case of the larger occupiers first, since the results obtained are found to apply *a fortiori* to the crofter class. There are three problems to be solved in the equitable hire of land: the amount of the rent, the length of the tenure and of the notice to quit, and the security for the disentanglement of the landlord's and the tenant's capital on the termination of the tenancy. Rent is properly a variable surplus determined by the excess of the price obtained for the produce over the expenses of production (including the ordinary rate of agricultural profits to the farmer), but in practice rent has come to be regarded as the price which the manufacturer of wool, beef, etc., pays for his raw material—

land. If this price is determined by competition, and is not merely a low customary price, it is absurd that it should be fixed for a long period; for the margin of profit is small, and the course of the seasons and of the prices of agricultural requisites and products is extremely uncertain. But Government cannot foresee these changes any better than the parties concerned, although by furnishing ample statistics it may enable them to arrive at a more correct conclusion; nor can the intervention of Government in fixing rent on the larger farms be justified on the ground of a natural inequality in the position of landlord and tenant; at the present time, indeed, the position of the tenant is probably the more favourable of the two for making a good bargain.

Again, as regards the length of tenure, there seems to be no necessity for interfering with private arrangements. Here, as in the case of rent, all that seems required is that the same general laws should apply to landlord and tenant alike; no exceptional security should be given to the landlord for rent unless, as in the French Code, the tenant is privileged when the crop is much below the average; if the tenant cannot transfer his lease without the landlord's consent, the landlord should not be allowed to transfer his land without giving the tenant the option of breaking the lease; and generally no law should remain in force which cannot be applied, *mutatis mutandis*, to either party.

But when we pass on to the length of the notice to quit, we cross the borders of non-intervention. As soon as a tenant has stocked a farm and brought on to it the necessary capital, he is no longer on the same footing as his landlord. If he has to remove suddenly the markets may be unfavourable, and he may not be able to obtain another suitable holding. Here, then, it seems desirable that the law should determine the minimum time of notice which the nature of the case seems to demand, and such interference can be justified by analogies from other branches of trade and industry. The principle is already admitted, and the only question is whether the time of notice now accorded should not be extended, and the example furnished by the best modern leases be universally followed.

But it is in regard to security for the tenant's capital that the necessity for the intervention of the State is most urgent. The existing law is grotesquely unfair to the tenant and indirectly injurious to the landlord and to the public. If a tenant is not allowed compensation for the capital he has annexed to the land, he will in the first place be inclined to risk as little as possible, and then, in case of removal, to extract as much as possible from the land by any process whatever. The desirability of compensation to some extent is now generally admitted, but there is still a divergence of opinion as to the degree to which in practice the principle should be carried. The line of division between cases for compensation and non-compensation has hitherto been generally decided according to the relative "permanence" of the improvements. But on analysis it appears that consent on the part of the landlord is demanded in the case of "permanent" improvements really on the ground that they might change the character of the subject; and it seems preferable to allow compensation for all capital necessary for good husbandry which, whether in a permanent form or not, does not change the nature of the holding. There is no infringement of proprietary rights, for the alterations in question only produce changes in value; if the value falls the landlord receives compensation from the tenant for deterioration, if it rises the tenant obtains an equitable share of the gain. The interest of the landlord is further protected by giving him in all cases the option of making the improvements, and when they are done by the tenant the compensation is calculated by the addition which the increased power of production has made to the old letting value (other things remaining the same), so that, even in this case, the landlord gains by anything which in future adds to the value of this increase in the produce. The natural method of adjusting compensation appears to be by arbiters chosen by the parties, and, *prima facie*, the appointment of official valuators does not appear to be necessary.

In the case of crofters the field of compensation should be further extended, and compensation given in all cases where improvements of any kind have been made to which the landlord is supposed to have given his consent by refraining from eviction. If the landlord does not wish waste land to be reclaimed, let him exercise his right of eviction if the tenant begins reclamations; but if he allows the tenant to remain, and enters only a formal protest, let him receive only a formal share in the value of the tenant's improvements. But the root from which all the difficulties of the crofter question spring is the size of the holdings, and there seems to be no reason why the principle of the factory legislation should not be applied, and the landlord, if he lets his land to crofters at all, be compelled to let it in such portions that an average industrious man may make a livelihood. With a reasonable notice to quit and security for the fruits of his labour, the crofter has nothing to fear from rack-renting; and larger holdings could pay a proportionately higher rent. The emigration of the surplus population would tend to raise the standard of comfort of the crofters to the level of other labourers, and with this improvement in their condition their labour would become more efficient and their husbandry more enterprising; as a consequence the rents of the small holdings would rise and the landlords be induced to increase their number. But to attempt either to restrain emigration, or to compel the landowners to establish suddenly a number of crofters on enlarged holdings without guarantees against subdivision, would be worse than useless. The small tenant of a holding that is not too small to afford full scope for his energy has always a natural protection against the larger tenant, for the former only expects the wages of his labour, whilst the latter expects also profits on his capital. If then the way is opened for the improvement of the crofters, the higher rent they can offer will ensure the extension of the class over suitable land, and even in this case the tenant's gain will not be the landlord's loss.

Edinburgh University Press:
T. AND A. CONSTABLE, PRINTERS TO HER MAJESTY.

15a Castle Street,
Edinburgh, *May* 1883.

LIST OF BOOKS

PUBLISHED BY DAVID DOUGLAS.

ADAMSON—On the Philosophy of Kant.

By Robert Adamson, M.A., Professor of Logic and Mental Philosophy, Owens College; formerly Examiner in Philosophy in the University of Edinburgh. Ex. fcap. 8vo, 6s.

"Within less than two hundred pages they convey to the intelligent reader a fair knowledge of Kant's method and doctrines. The notes indicate wide reading, and form an admirable appendix to the text."—*Theological Quarterly.*

AGNEW—The Correspondence of Sir Patrick Waus of Barnbarroch, during the latter half of the Sixteenth Century, from original in the Family Charter-Chest. Edited by R. Vans Agnew. 1 vol. demy 8vo, 21s.

ALEXANDER—Johnny Gibb of Gushetneuk in the Parish of Pyketillim, with Glimpses of Parish Politics about A.D. 1843. By William Alexander. Sixth Edition, with Glossary, ex. fcap. 8vo, 2s.

Seventh Edition, with Twenty Illustrations—Portraits and Landscapes—by George Reid, R.S.A. Demy 8vo, 10s. 6d.

"A most vigorous and truthful delineation of local character, drawn from a portion of the country where that character is peculiarly worthy of careful study and record."—*The Right Hon. W. E. Gladstone.*

"It is a grand addition to our pure Scottish dialect; . . . it is not merely a capital specimen of genuine Scottish northern *dialect;* but it is a capital specimen of pawky characteristic Scottish humour. It is full of good hard Scottish dry fun."—*Dean Ramsay.*

ALEXANDER—Life among my Ain Folk.

1. Mary Malcolmson's Wee Maggie.
2. Couper Sandy.
3. Francie Herriegerie's Sharger Laddie.
4. Baubie Huie's Bastard Geet.
5. Glengillodram.

Ex. fcap. 8vo. Second Edition. Cloth, 2s. 6d. Paper, 2s.

"Mr. Alexander thoroughly understands the position of men and women who are too often treated with neglect, and graphically depicts their virtues and vices, and shows to his readers difficulties, struggles, and needs which they are sure to be the wiser for taking into view."—*Freeman.*

"'Baubie Huie's Bastard Geet,' which is full of quiet but effective humour, is the clearest revelation we have ever seen of the feeling in Scotch country districts in regard to certain aspects of morality."—*Spectator.*

ALEXANDER—Notes and Sketches of Northern Rural Life in the Eighteenth Century, by the Author of "Johnny Gibb of Gushetneuk." In 1 vol. ex. fcap. 8vo, 2s.

"This delightful little volume. It is a treasure. . . . We admire the telling simplicity of the style, the sly, pawky, Aberdonian humour, the wide acquaintance with the social and other conditions of the northern rural counties of last century, and the fund of illustrative anecdotes which enrich the volume. The author has done great service to the cause of history and of progress. It is worth a great many folios of the old dry-as-dust type."—*Daily Review.*

ANDERSON—The Gallop.

By E. L. ANDERSON. Illustrated by Instantaneous Photography. 1 vol. fcap. 4to, 2s. 6d.

"Mr. E. L. Anderson has collected in a thin little book, admirably illustrated by Mr. Muybridge's system of photography, all that theory and practice can teach us as to how a horse should be trained to gallop."—*Saturday Review.*

"It cannot fail to be of value to the riding and sporting world."—*American Register.*

ANDERSON—Scotland in Early Christian Times.

By JOSEPH ANDERSON, LL.D., Keeper of the National Museum of the Antiquaries of Scotland. 1 vol. demy 8vo, with Eighty-four Wood Engravings, and Three Quarto Diagrams of Celtic Ornamentations. In 1 vol. demy 8vo, price 12s. (Being the Rhind Lectures in Archæology, 1879.)

"We know of no work within the reach of all students so completely realising its professions, and we can confidently recommend to the architect, artist, and antiquary, young and old, this volume on Celtic art in Scotland."—*British Architect and Engineer.*

"Mr. Anderson sets the facts forth with an accuracy too rare in works of this class, and arranges them in the light of principles that make many of them for the first time intelligible."—*St. James's Gazette.*

ANDERSON—Scotland in Early Christian Times.

Second Series. Celtic Art. By JOSEPH ANDERSON, LL.D., Keeper of the Museum of Antiquities, Edinburgh. 1 vol. demy 8vo, price 12s. (Being the Rhind Lectures in Archæology, 1880.)

"All interested in the development of art will find here much new material for reflection."—*Westminster Review.*

ANDERSON—Scotland in Pagan Times. The Iron Age.

By JOSEPH ANDERSON, LL.D. 1 vol. demy 8vo, price 12s. (Being the Rhind Lectures in Archæology, 1881.)

ARMSTRONG—The History of Liddesdale, Eskdale, Ewes-dale, Wauchopedale, and the Debateable Land. Part I. from the Twelfth Century to 1530. By ROBERT BRUCE ARMSTRONG. The edition will be limited to 275 copies demy quarto, and 105 copies on large paper (10 inches by 13). With an Appendix of 70 Documents, arranged in Chronological order down to 1566. The selection has been made from private Charter-chests, MS. collections in London and Edinburgh, and rare printed works, and comprises Charters, Rent-rolls, Excerpts from the Accounts of the Lord High Treasurer, Bonds of Manrent, Bonds for the Re-entry of Prisoners, Lists of Scottish Borderers under English Assurance, Injuries inflicted by the English and by the Scottish Borderers under English Assurance from September 1543 to June 1544, interesting Letters and a Military Report on the West March of Scotland and Liddesdale by an English official, etc. etc.

The Volume will be illustrated by Maps, Etchings, Lithographs, and Woodcuts, all of which, with the exception of Blaeu's Maps of Liddesdale and Eskdale, and

the etchings of James IV., James V., and the Earl of Angus, by C. Lawrie—will either be from the author's drawings or wholly executed by himself The lithographs in colour will include facsimiles of four interesting representations of Scottish Border Castles and Towns drawn between the years 1563 and 1566, Plates of Arms of the Lords of Liddesdale, of the Clans of the District, of Lindsay of Wauchope, also of the Seals of John Armstrong and William Elliot, etc. etc.
[In the Press, to be ready in November.

BAILDON—Morning Clouds:

Being divers Poems by H. B. Baildon, B.A. Cantab., Author of "Rosamund," etc. Ex. fcap. 8vo, 5s.

"Their tremulous beauty, delicate fancies, and wealth of language, recall the poetry of Shelley."—*Literary World.*

BAILDON—First Fruits. 5s.

BAILDON—Rosamund. 5s.

Bible Readings.

Extra fcap. 8vo, 2s.

BISHOP—The Voyage of the Paper Canoe.

A Geographical Journey of 2500 Miles, from Quebec to the Gulf of Mexico, during the year 1874-75. By N. H. Bishop. With Maps and Plates, 10s. 6d.

"There are some capital stories in this book, with a racy American flavour; and Mr. Bishop especially shines in his delineation of the liberated and enfranchised negro."—*Pall Mall Gazette.*

BLACKIE—Lyrical Poems.

Crown 8vo, cloth, 7s. 6d.

BLACKIE—The Language and Literature of the Scottish Highlands. In 1 vol. crown 8vo, 6s.

"The way to a mother's heart is through her children; the way to a people's heart is through its language."—*Jean Paul Richter.*

"Ein Buch, das ich auch deutschen Lesern, und zwar in einem beträchtlich weitem Umfange, nicht angelegentlich genug empfehlen kann."—*Dr. R. Pauli.*

BLACKIE—Four Phases of Morals:

Socrates, Aristotle, Christianity, and Utilitarianism. Lectures delivered before the Royal Institution, London. Ex. fcap. 8vo, Second Edition, 5s.

BLACKIE—Songs of Religion and Life.

Fcap. 8vo, 6s.

BLACKIE—On Self-Culture:

Intellectual, Physical, and Moral. A *Vade-Mecum* for Young Men and Students. Fourteenth Edition. Fcap. 8vo, 2s. 6d.

"Every parent should put it into the hands of his son."—*Scotsman.*

"Students in all countries would do well to take as their *vade-mecum* a little book on self-culture by the eminent Professor of Greek in the University of Edinburgh."—*Medical Press and Circular.*

"An invaluable manual to be put into the hands of students and young men." —*Era.*

"Written in that lucid and nervous prose of which he is a master."—*Spectator.*

"An adequate guide to a generous, eager, and sensible life."—*Academy.*

"The volume is a little thing, but it is a *multum in parvo* . . . a little locket gemmed within and without with real stones fitly set."—*Courant.*

BLACKIE—On Greek Pronunciation.
Demy 8vo, 3s. 6d.

BLACKIE—On Beauty.
Crown 8vo, cloth, 8s. 6d.

BLACKIE—Musa Burschicosa.
A Book of Songs for Students and University Men. Fcap. 8vo, 2s. 6d.

BLACKIE—War Songs of the Germans.
Fcap. 8vo, price 2s. 6d. cloth; 2s. paper.

BLACKIE—Political Tracts.
No. 1. GOVERNMENT. No. 2. EDUCATION. Price 1s. each.

BLACKIE—Gaelic Societies.
Highland Depopulation and Land Law Reform. Demy 8vo, 6d.

BLACKIE—Homer and the Iliad.
In three Parts. 4 vols. demy 8vo, price 42s.

BOWEN—"Verily, Verily," The Amens of Christ.
By the Rev. GEORGE BOWEN of Bombay. Small 4to, cloth, 5s.

"For private and devotional reading this book will be found very helpful and stimulative."—*Literary World.*

BOWEN—Daily Meditations by Rev. G. Bowen of Bombay.
With Introductory Notice by Rev. W. HANNA, D.D., Author of "The Last Day of our Lord's Passion." New Edition, small 4to, cloth, 5s.

"Among such books we shall scarcely find another which exhibits the same freshness and vividness of idea, the same fervour of faith, the same intensity or devotion. . . . I count it a privilege to introduce in this country a book so fitted to attract and to benefit."—*Extract from Preface.*

"These meditations are the production of a missionary whose mental history is very remarkable. . . . His conversion to a religious life is undoubtedly one of the most remarkable on record. They are all distinguished by a tone of true piety, and are wholly free from a sectarian or controversial bias."—*Morning Post.*

BROWN—Horæ Subsecivæ. First Series.
By JOHN BROWN, M.D. In 1 vol. crown 8vo. Fourth Edition, with a Portrait by JAS. FAED, 7s. 6d. Containing—

Locke and Sydenham.
Dr. Andrew Combe.
Dr. Henry Marshall and Military Hygiene.
Art and Science: A Contrasted Parallel.
Our Gideon Grays.
Dr. Andrew Brown and Sydenham.
Free Competition in Medicine.
Edward Forbes.
Dr. Adams, of Banchory.
Henry Vaughan.
Excursus Ethicus.
Professor Syme.
Dr. John Scott.
Sir Robert Christison.
Lectures on Health.

"The whole volume is full of wit and wisdom. . . . It will be a medical classic like the "Religio Medici."—*Edinburgh Medical Journal.*

BROWN—Horæ Subsecivæ. Second Series.

By JOHN BROWN, M.D. In 1 vol. crown 8vo. Eleventh Edition, 7s. 6d. Containing—

Letter to John Cairns, D.D.
Dr. Chalmers.
Dr. George Wilson.
Her Last Half-Crown.
Queen Mary's Child-Garden.
Our Dogs.
Notes on Art.
"Oh, I'm Wat, Wat!"
Education Through the Senses.

ΑΓΧΙΝΟΙΑ—Nearness of the ΝΟΥΣ—Presence of Mind—'ΕΥΣΤΟΧΙΑ: Happy Guessing.

The Black Dwarf's Bones.
Rab and his Friends.
"With Brains, Sir!"
Arthur H. Hallam.

"He speaks to us out of the riches of a storied past with all the charm of one who knew and loved it well; and his manner is so sympathetic, and his touch so gentle and exquisite, that we always feel he knows and loves the present with the truest and largest of hearts."—*Literary World.*

BROWN—Horæ Subsecivæ. Third Series.

By JOHN BROWN, M.D. In 1 vol. crown 8vo. Fourth Edition, with a Portrait by GEO. REID, R.S.A., 7s. 6d. Containing—

John Leech.
A Jacobite Family.
Mystifications.
Miss Stirling Graham of Duntrune.
Thackeray's Death.
Marjorie Fleming.
Minchmoor.
"In Clear Dream and Solemn Vision."
Jeems the Doorkeeper.
Sir E. Landseer's Picture, "There's Life in the Old Dog Yet," &c.
The Enterkin.
The Duke of Athole.
Struan.
Dick *Miki*, or *Cur*, why?
E. V. K. to his Friend in Town.
Sir Henry Raeburn.
Something about a Well, With more of our Dogs.

"Dr. John Brown's humour, pathos, and geniality are acknowledged qualities. . . . We end with a hearty recommendation of the book to readers of almost every variety of taste, for they will find here scores of stories which will make them laugh or shudder, or feel a great disposition to cry."—*Saturday Review.*

"In this new volume of the 'Horæ Subsecivæ' Dr. John Brown has given us some more of his pleasant and discursive essays on men and beasts."—*Pall Mall Gazette.*

"One very obvious characteristic of these papers is their appearance of ease and spontaneity. They impress us as the work of one full of his subject and delighted with it."—*Academy.*

"With two exceptions the essays and sketches are all racy of the northern soil."—*St. James's Gazette.*

"The author of 'Rab and his Friends' has published a volume of stray papers in which many delightful glimpses will be found of old Edinburgh society."—*Dundee Advertiser.*

"To see another work of Dr. John Brown is pleasant unto the eyes as to see the face of an old friend."—*Scotsman.*

"There is in almost every one of Dr. Brown's inimitable papers such an 'eeriness' as befitteth best only the hours of darkness."—*Spectator.*

"He has not a little of Mr. Ruskin's love of nature, but his humour and his wide human affections preserve him from the evils of over intensity."—*Nonconformist.*

"The author of 'Rab and his Friends' has a place apart among contemporary essayists. His manner and his matter are alike peculiar to himself."—*Athenæum.*

Separate Papers, extracted from "Horæ Subsecivæ."

Rab and his Friends.

With India-proof portrait of the Author after Faed, and seven India-proof Illustrations after Sir G. Harvey, Sir J. Noel Paton, Mrs. Blackburn, and G. Reid, R.S.A. Demy 4to, cloth, 9s.

Rab and his Friends.

Cheap Illustrated Edition. Square 12mo, ornamental wrapper, 1s.

Rab and his Friends.

Sixty-fourth Thousand. Price 6d.

Our Dogs.

Twentieth Thousand. Price 6d.

"With Brains, Sir!"

Seventh Thousand. Price 6d.

Minchmoor.

Tenth Thousand. Price 6d.

The Enterkin.

Seventh Thousand. Price 6d.

Jeems the Doorkeeper.

Twelfth Thousand. Price 6d.

Marjorie Fleming: A Sketch.

Sixteenth Thousand. Price 6d.

Plain Words on Health.

Twenty-seventh Thousand. Price 6d.

Something about a Well: With more of our Dogs. Price 6d.

Arthur H. Hallam.

Price 2s. sewed; and 2s. 6d. cloth, gilt edges.

Supplementary Chapter to the Life of the Rev. John Brown, D.D. Second Edition. Price 2s.

BROWN—The Capercaillie in Scotland.

By J. A. Harvie Brown. Etchings on Copper, and Map illustrating the extension of its range since its Restoration at Taymouth in 1837 and 1838. Demy 8vo, 8s. 6d.

"To no one will it prove uninteresting, and to ornithologists and sportsmen it is specially inviting."—*Dundee Advertiser.*

"A carefully prepared and exhaustive monograph of the Capercailzie in Scotland, which ought to be perused by every proprietor of an estate, forester, and naturalist in the country."—*Journal of Forestry.*

BULLOCH—George Jamesone. The Scottish Vandyke.

1587 to 1644. By John Bulloch. With Two Illustrations by George Reid, R.S.A. [*In the Press.*

BURNETT—"The Red Book of Menteith" Reviewed.

By George Burnett, Advocate, Lyon King of Arms. In 1 vol. small 4to, 5s.

BURROUGHS—Winter Sunshine.

By John Burroughs. 32mo, 1s., and cloth 2s.

"The minuteness of his observation, the keenness of his perception, give him a real originality, and his sketches have a delightful oddity, vivacity, and freshness."—*The Nation (New York).*

CABLE—Old Creole Days.

By GEO. W. CABLE. 32mo, 1s.; and in cloth, 2s.

"The combination of grotesque humour and of genuine pathos is most charming, and quite unique and inimitable."—*Glasgow Citizen.*

CAIRNS—Memoir of John Brown, D.D.

By JOHN CAIRNS, D.D., Berwick-on-Tweed. Crown 8vo, 7s. 6d.

CAMPBELL—My Indian Journal.

Containing Descriptions of the principal Field Sports of India, with Notes on the Natural History and Habits of the Wild Animals of the Country. By Colonel WALTER CAMPBELL, Author of "The Old Forest Ranger." 8vo, with Illustrations by Wolf, 16s.

CHALMERS—Life and Works of Rev. Thomas Chalmers, D.D., LL.D.

MEMOIRS OF THE REV. THOMAS CHALMERS. By Rev. W. HANNA, D.D., LL.D. New Edition. 2 vols. crown 8vo, cloth, 12s.

DAILY SCRIPTURE READINGS. Cheap Edition. 2 vols. crown 8vo, 10s.

ASTRONOMICAL DISCOURSES, 1s.

COMMERCIAL DISCOURSES, 1s.

SELECT WORKS, in 12 vols. crown 8vo, cloth, per vol. 6s.

Lectures on the Romans. 2 vols.
Sermons. 2 vols.
Natural Theology, Lectures on Butler's Analogy, etc. 1 vol.
Christian Evidences, Lectures on Paley's Evidences, etc. 1 vol.
Institutes of Theology. 2 vols.
Political Economy, with Cognate Essays. 1 vol.
Polity of a Nation. 1 vol.
Church and College Establishments. 1 vol.
Moral Philosophy, Introductory Essays, Index, etc. 1 vol.

CHIENE—Lectures on Surgical Anatomy.

By JOHN CHIENE, M.D., Prof. of Surgery in the University of Edinburgh. In 1 vol. 8vo. With numerous illustrations drawn on Stone by BERJEAU. 12s. 6d.

"Dr. Chiene has succeeded in going over the most important part of the ground, and in a pleasant readable manner. . . . They (the plates) are well executed, and considerably enhance the value of the book."—*Lancet.*

"The book will be a great help to both teachers and taught, and students can depend upon the teaching as being sound."—*Medical Times and Gazette.*

CHIENE—Lectures on the Elements or First Principles of Surgery. By JOHN CHIENE, M.D., Prof. of Surgery in the University of Edinburgh. Demy 8vo, 2s. 6d.

CHRISTIE—Traditional Ballad Airs.

Arranged and Harmonised for the Pianoforte and Harmonium. By W. CHRISTIE, M.A., and the late WILLIAM CHRISTIE, Monquhitter. Vols. I. and II. 42s. each.

"As a contribution to our national stories it takes rank perhaps even above Dean Ramsay's popular 'Reminiscences of Scottish Life and Character.'"—*Inverness Courier.*

CONSTABLE—Archibald Constable and his Literary Correspondents: a Memorial. By his Son, THOMAS CONSTABLE. 3 vols. 8vo, 36s., with Portrait.

"He (Mr. Constable) was a genius in the publishing world. . . . The creator of the Scottish publishing trade."—*Times.*

"These three volumes are of a singular and lasting interest."—*Nonconformist.*

CRAWFORD—The Earldom of Mar, in Sunshine and in Shade, during Five Hundred Years. With incidental Notices of the leading Cases of Scottish Dignities of King Charles I. till now. By ALEXANDER, Earl of Crawford and Balcarres, LORD LINDSAY, etc. etc. 2 vols. demy 8vo, 32s.

"It is one of the most learned expositions of peerage history and peerage law, which it has been our fortune to find."—*Morning Post.*

CROOM—A Clinical and Experimental Study of the Bladder during Parturition. By J. H. CROOM, M.B., F.R.C.P.E. Small 4to, with Illustrations. [*In the Press.*

CUMMING—Wild Men and Wild Beasts.

Adventures in Camp and Jungle. By Lieut.-Colonel GORDON CUMMING. With Illustrations by Lieut.-Col. BAIGRIE and others. Second Edition. Demy 4to, price 24s.

Also, a cheaper edition, with *Lithographic* Illustrations. 8vo, 12s.

DASENT—Burnt Njal.

From the Icelandic of the Njal's Saga. By Sir GEORGE WEBBE DASENT, D.C.L. 2 vols. demy 8vo, with Maps and Plans, 28s.

DASENT—Gisli the Outlaw.

From the Icelandic. By Sir GEORGE WEBBE DASENT, D.C.L. Small 4to, with Illustrations, 7s. 6d.

DASENT—Tales from the Norse.

By Sir GEORGE WEBBE DASENT, D.C.L. Third Edition, with Introduction and Appendix. In 1 vol. demy 8vo. [*In the Press.*

DAVIDSON—Inverurie and the Earldom of the Garioch.

A Topographical and Historical Account of the Garioch from the Earliest Times to the Revolution Settlement, with a Genealogical Appendix of Garioch Families flourishing at the Period of the Revolution Settlement and still represented. By the Rev. JOHN DAVIDSON, D.D., Minister of Inverurie. In 1 vol. 4to, 25s.

DAY—The Uses and Manufacture of Iron and Steel, from Prehistoric Ages to the Present Time. By ST. JOHN V. DAY, C.E., F.R.S.E., F.S.A. (Scot.), Member of the Iron and Steel Institute, Member of the Institution of Mechanical Engineers, Associate of the Institution of Civil Engineers, Member of Council of the Institute of Patent Agents, etc. To be complete in 3 vols. demy 8vo. (Vol. I. in October.) [*In the Press.*

DITTMAR—A Manual of Chemical Analysis.

By Professor WILLIAM DITTMAR. Ex. fcap. 8vo, 5s.

DITTMAR—Tables for Do.

Demy 8vo, 3s. 6d.

DUN—Veterinary Medicines; their Actions and Uses.

By FINLAY DUN. Sixth Edition, revised and enlarged. Demy 8vo, 15s.

DUNBAR -Social Life in Former Days;

Chiefly in the Province of Moray. Illustrated by Letters and Family Papers. By E. DUNBAR DUNBAR, late Captain 21st Fusiliers. 2 vols. demy 8vo, 19s. 6d.

ERSKINE—Letters of Thomas Erskine of Linlathen.

Edited by WILLIAM HANNA, D.D., Author of the "Memoirs of Dr. Chalmers," etc. Third Edition. In 1 vol. crown 8vo, 9s.

"Here is one who speaks out of the fulness of a large living human heart; whose words will awaken an echo in the hearts of many burdened with the cares of time, perplexed with the movements of the spirit of our time, who will speak to their deepest needs, and lead them to a haven of rest."—*Daily Review.*

"It does one good to come in contact with so saintly a man, and Dr. Hanna has certainly conferred a benefit on the Church at large by editing this volume."—*Edinburgh Courant.*

"'How high must that peak have been which caught the light so early,' were the words with which a writer in the *Contemporary Review*, in sketching the life of Thomas Erskine, shortly after his death, characterised his position, his spirit, and his influence."—*Nonconformist.*

ERSKINE—The Internal Evidence of Revealed Religion.

Crown 8vo, 5s.

"Before Mr. Erskine went abroad in 1822, he published his first work on 'The Internal Evidence of Revealed Religion,' in which he pursued in a more extended manner something of the same line of thought as that already spoken of. HIS GREAT AIM WAS TO SHOW THE DIVINE ORIGIN OF CHRISTIANITY BOTH FROM THE FITTING ILLUSTRATION WHICH IT FURNISHED OF THE CHARACTER OF GOD AND ITS BEARING ON THE CHARACTER OF MAN, to demonstrate that its facts not only present an impressive exhibition of all the moral qualities which can be conceived to reside in the Divine mind, but also contain all those objects which have a natural tendency to excite and suggest in the human mind that combination of moral feelings which has been termed moral perfection."—*Edinburgh Review.*

ERSKINE—The Unconditional Freeness of the Gospel.

New Edition, revised. Crown 8vo, 3s. 6d.

ERSKINE—The Spiritual Order,

And other Papers selected from the MSS. of the late THOMAS ERSKINE of Linlathen. Second Edition. Crown 8vo, 5s.

"It will for a few have a value which others will not the least understand. But all must recognise in it the utterance of a spirit profoundly penetrated with the sense of brotherhood, and with the claims of common humanity."—*Spectator.*

"Very deserving of study."—*Times.*

Vide BIBLE READINGS and FRAGMENTS OF TRUTH.

ERSKINE—The Doctrine of Election,

And its Connection with the General Tenor of Christianity, illustrated especially from the Epistle to the Romans. Pp. xxiv. and 318. Second Edition. Crown 8vo, 6s.

ERSKINE—The Brazen Serpent:

Or, Life coming through Death. Third Edition. 5s.

FERGUSON—Guide to the Great North of Scotland Railway. By W. FERGUSON of Kinmundy. In 1 vol. crown 8vo; in paper cover, 1s.; cloth cover, 1s. 6d.

"An extremely readable and amusing, as well as instructive, little volume.'—*Aberdeen Free Press.*

FERGUSON—Twelve Sketches of Scenery and Antiquities on the Line of the Great North of Scotland Railway By GEORGE REID, R.S.A. With Illustrative Letterpress by W. FERGUSON of Kinmundy. Folio. [*In the Press.*

FLETCHER—Autobiography of Mrs. Fletcher

(Of Edinburgh), with Letters and other Family Memorials. Edited by her Daughter. Second Edition. Crown 8vo, 7s. 6d.

"This is a delightful book. It contains an illustrative record of a singularly noble, true, pure, prolonged, and happy life. The story is recounted with a candour, vivacity, and grace which are very charming."—*Daily Review.*

FLEURY—L'Histoire de France.

Par M. LAMÉ FLEURY. New Edition. 18mo, cloth, 2s. 6d.

FORBES—The Deepening of the Spiritual Life.

By A. P. FORBES, D.C.L., Bishop of Brechin. Fifth Edition. Calf, red edges, 3s. 6d.

FORBES—Kalendars of Scottish Saints,

With Personal Notices of those of Alba, etc. By ALEXANDER PENROSE FORBES, D.C.L., Bishop of Brechin. 1 vol. 4to, price £3 : 3s. A few copies for sale on large paper, £5 : 15 : 6.

"A truly valuable contribution to the archæology of Scotland."—*Guardian.*

"We must not forget to thank the author for the great amount of information he has put together, and for the labour he has bestowed on a work which can never be remunerative."—*Saturday Review.*

"His laborious and very interesting work on the early Saints of Alba, Laudonia, and Strathclyde."—*Quarterly Review.*

FORBES—Missale Drummondiense. The Ancient Irish Missal in the possession of the Baroness Willoughby d'Eresby. Edited by the Rev. G. H. FORBES. Half-morocco, demy 8vo, 12s.

Fragments of Truth.

Being the Exposition of several Passages of Scripture. Third Edition. Extra fcap. 8vo, 5s.

FRASER—Alcohol: its Function and Place.

By THOMAS R. FRASER, M.D., F.R.S., Professor of Materia Medica in the University of Edinburgh. With Diagrams and Tables. 8vo, 1s.

GAIRDNER and SPEDDING—Studies in English History.

By JAMES GAIRDNER and JAMES SPEDDING. In 1 vol. demy 8vo, 12s.

1. THE LOLLARDS.
2. SIR JOHN FALSTAFF.
3. KATHERINE OF ARRAGON'S FIRST AND SECOND MARRIAGES.
4. CASE OF SIR THOMAS OVERBURY.
5. DIVINE RIGHT OF KINGS.
6. SUNDAY, ANCIENT AND MODERN.

"The authors' names alone are a sufficient guarantee that the Essays in this beautifully printed volume were worth reprinting."—*St. James's Gazette.*

"It will enlighten the readers on some points in respect to which they are at present very much in the dark."—*Scotsman.*

GAIRDNER—On Medicine and Medical Education.
By W. T. GAIRDNER, Professor of the Practice of Medicine in the University of Glasgow. Three Lectures, with Notes and an Appendix. 8vo, 3s. 6d.

GAIRDNER—Clinical and Pathological Notes on Pericarditis. By W. T. GAIRDNER, Professor of the Practice of Medicine in the University of Glasgow. 8vo, sewed, 1s.

Gifts for Men.
By X. H. Crown 8vo, 6s.

"There is hardly a living theologian who might not be proud to claim many of her thoughts as his own."—*Glasgow Herald.*

GILFILLAN—Sketches Literary and Theological;
Being selections from the unpublished MSS. of the Rev. GEORGE GILFILLAN. Edited by FRANK HENDERSON, Esq., M.P. 7s. 6d.

"The papers chosen for publication are chiefly critical, and they form a most readable, instructive, and interesting volume."—*Dundee Advertiser.*

GORDON—The Roof of the World;
Being the Narrative of a Journey over the High Plateau of Tibet to the Russian Frontier, and the Oxus Sources on Pamir. By Lieut.-Col. T. E. GORDON, C.S.I. With numerous Illustrations. Royal 8vo, 31s. 6d.

GORDON—The Home Life of Sir David Brewster.
By his Daughter, Mrs. GORDON. Second Edition. Crown 8vo, 6s.

"With his own countrymen it is sure of a welcome, and to the *savants* of Europe, and of the New World, it will have a real and special interest of its own."—*Pall Mall Gazette.*

Also a cheaper Edition, crown 8vo, 2s. 6d.

By the same Author.

GORDON—Workers.
Fourth Thousand. Fcap. 8vo, limp cloth, 1s.

GORDON—Work;
Or, Plenty to do and How to do it. Thirty-fifth Thousand. Fcap. 8vo, cloth, 2s. 6d.

Warfare Work.
Everyday Work.
Social Work.
Home Work.
Single Women's Work.
Waiting Work.
Preparatory Work.
Desultory Work.
Praising Work.
Special Work.
Praying Work.
Homely Hints about Work.
Reward of Work.
Future Work.
Combined Work.
Little Children's Work.
Young Ladies' Work.
Work of Teachers and Taught.
Household Work.
Work of Employers and Employed.
Country Work.
Sabbath Work.
Thought Work.
Proving Work
Rest.

"Mrs. Gordon is precisely one of the ladies for the time,—not a drowsy dreamer, but fully awake, strong in heart, ardent in zeal, and intent on the vigorous use of right means to promote right ends."—*British Banner.*

GORDON—Little Millie and her Four Places.
Cheap Edition. Fifty-eighth Thousand. Limp cloth, 1s.

"The narrative is simple and attractive; the plan of the work is well conceived; the style is fluent and lively; and the interest of the tale is well sustained to the close."—*Spectator.*

GORDON—Sunbeams in the Cottage;

Or, What Women may do. A Narrative chiefly addressed to the Working Classes. Cheap Edition. Forty-fourth Thousand. Limp cloth, 1s.

"The fruit alike of strong sense and philanthropic genius. . . . There is in every chapter much to instruct the mind as well as to mould the heart and to mend the manners. The volume has all the charms of romance, while every page is stamped with utility."—*Christian Witness.*

GORDON—Prevention;

Or, An Appeal to Economy and Common Sense. 8vo, 6d.

GORDON—The Word and the World.

Twelfth Edition. Price 2d.

GORDON—Leaves of Healing for the Sick and Sorrowful.

Cheap Edition, limp cloth, 2s.

GORDON—The Motherless Boy;

With an Illustration by Sir J. Noel Paton, R.S.A. Cheap Edition, limp cloth, 1s.

"Alike in manner and matter calculated to attract youthful attention, and to attract it by the best of all means—sympathy."—*Scotsman.*

GORDON—Our Daughters.

An Account of the Young Women's Christian Association and Institute Union. Price 2d.

GORDON—Hay Macdowall Grant of Arndilly; his Life,

Labours, and Teaching. New and Cheaper Edition. 1 vol. crown 8vo, limp cloth, 2s. 6d.

HANNA—The Life of our Lord.

By the Rev. William Hanna, D.D., LL.D. 6 vols., handsomely bound in cloth extra, gilt edges, 30s.

Separate vols., cloth extra, gilt edges, 5s. each.

1. The Earlier Years of our Lord. Fifth Edition.
2. The Ministry in Galilee. Fourth Edition.
3. The Close of the Ministry. Sixth Thousand.
4. The Passion Week. Sixth Thousand.
5. The Last Day of our Lord's Passion. Twenty-third Edition.
6. The Forty Days after the Resurrection. Eighth Edition.

"If Dr. Hanna excels in one thing more than another, it is in the simplicity of his style. It is this quality which gives beauty and force to the work before us. One cannot proceed far into the pages of this Life of our Lord without being struck with the unbroken continuity of movement illustrative of the life and work of Christ."—*Christian Union.*

HANNA—The Resurrection of the Dead.

By William Hanna, D.D., LL.D. Second Edition. One vol. fcap. 8vo, 5s.

HASTIE—Protestant Missions to the Heathen. A General

Survey of their Present State throughout the World. By Prof. Th. Christlieb. Translated from the German by Rev. W. Hastie, Calcutta. 1 vol. demy 8vo, 1s.

HASTIE—Elements of Philosophy.

Part First. 1s.

HASTIE—The Perpetuity of the Faith as our Ground of

Hope. 1s.

HODGSON—Errors in the Use of English.

Illustrated from the Writings of English Authors, from the Fourteenth Century to Our Own Time. By the late W. B. Hodgson, LL.D., Professor of Political Economy in the University of Edinburgh. Fourth Edition. 1 vol. crown 8vo, 3s. 6d.

"Those who most need such a book as Dr. Hodgson's will probably be the last to look into it. It will certainly amuse its readers, and will probably teach them a good deal which they did not know, or at least never thought about, before."—*The Saturday Review.*

"Perhaps at no period in the history of our language was such a work as this needed so much as it is at present. . . . It would save the feelings of many a lover of pure English were all forced, as a preliminary exercise, simply to read Professor Hodgson's collections of 'Errors in English.'"—*N.B. Daily Mail.*

"Beyond all doubt, Professor Hodgson has attained his object—viz. to set forth the merits of correctness in English composition by furnishing examples of the demerits of incorrectness—to bring home the abstract rule that a sentence must be lucid in order and logical in sequence."—*The Athenæum.*

"This little volume will surely do excellent service, and we strongly recommend it for the study of all."—*Manchester Examiner.*

"This posthumous work of Dr. Hodgson's deserves a hearty welcome, for it is sure to do good service for the object it has in view."—*The Academy.*

"His conversation, as every one who had the pleasure of his acquaintance knows, sparkled with anecdote and epigram, and not a little of the lustre and charm of his talk shines out of those pages."—*The Scotsman.*

"The book is neither large nor expensive, but it contains a great amount of careful and scholarly criticism."—*Aberdeen Free Press.*

"No one who aims at a pure style of English composition should be without this book."—*The Educational News.*

HODGSON—Life and Letters of the late W. B. Hodgson,

Professor of Political Economy in the University of Edinburgh. 1 vol. crown 8vo. [*In the Press.*

HOLMES—The Autocrat of the Breakfast-Table.

By Oliver Wendell Holmes. New and Revised Edition, containing fresh Preface and Bibliographical Notes by the Author. Printed at the Riverside Press. Crown 8vo, 10s. 6d.

HOLMES—The Professor at the Breakfast-Table.

New Edition. [*In the Press.*

HOLMES—The Poet at the Breakfast-Table.

By Oliver Wendell Holmes, M.D. New Edition, carefully Revised, with New Preface. Printed at the Riverside Press from New Electrotype Plates. With a Steel Portrait of the Author. Crown 8vo, 10s. 6d. [*Nearly ready.*

"As he is everybody's favourite, there is no occasion for critics to meddle with him, either to censure or to praise. He can afford to laugh at the whole reviewing fraternity. His wit is all his own, so sly and tingling, but without a drop of ill-nature in it, and never leaving a sting behind. His humour is so grotesque and queer that it reminds one of the frolics of Puck ; and deep pathos mingles with it so naturally that when the reader's eyes are brimming with tears he knows not whether they have their source in sorrow or in laughter."—*North American Review.*

HOME—Traces in Scotland of Ancient Water Lines, Marine,

Lacustrine, and Fluviatile. By David Milne-Home, LL.D., F.R.S.E. 1 vol. demy 8vo, 3s. 6d.

"To the student of geology and archæology the volume will present a compendium of precise and authentic observations, the importance of which cannot well be overrated, while for the general reader it contains a wonderfully interesting story of ceaseless change and vicissitude."—*Glasgow Herald.*

HOPE—A Sketch of the Life of George Hope of Fenton Barns. Compiled by his DAUGHTER. 6s.

Published with the sanction of the Author.

HOWELLS—A Modern Instance: A Novel.

By W. D. HOWELLS. Copyright Edition, in 2 vols. crown 8vo, 12s.

"What interests us throughout is the vivid picture of American social life as it really is."—*Spectator.*

"In 'A Modern Instance' Mr. Howells is as pitiless as life itself. As a piece of artistic work it cannot easily be surpassed."—*St. James's Gazette.*

"Among the books which treat of the lives of Americans at home the most remarkable is the 'Modern Instance.' It is more powerful than any of Mr. Howells's previous works."—*Blackwood's Magazine.*

'No one can call this book either pious or didactic fiction, but we have seldom met with a more religion-teaching book."—*The Guardian (London).*

"'A Modern Instance' is before all things a study of character."—*Athenæum.*

HOWELLS—Dr. Breen's Practice: A Novel.

Copyright Edition, in 1 vol. crown 8vo, 2s. 6d., or in cloth, 3s. 6d.

"In Dr. Breen's Practice we have an entertaining representation of modern American life, lightly and delicately touched off in Mr. Howells's peculiar style."—*Literary World.*

HOWELLS—A Woman's Reason: A Novel.

In crown 8vo. [*In the Press.*

By the same Author.

Pocket Editions in One Shilling Volumes. Calico, 1s. 6*d.; cloth gilt,* 2s.

HOWELLS—A Foregone Conclusion.

"It is the greatest triumph of the artist that out of material so little idealised he should have produced a story of such enduring and pathetic interest."—*The Times.*

HOWELLS—Their Wedding Journey.

"With just enough of story and dialogue to give to it the interest of a novel. It is also one of the most charming books of travel that we have ever seen."—*Christian Register (Boston).*

HOWELLS—A Chance Acquaintance.

"The bright, courageous, light-hearted realism of the whole, the gay charm of the principal characters, the refined humour of some of the incidents, the sentiment and style in which the pretty sparkling story is, as it were, embedded, were such as showed a new artistic force at work, and announced a great and original talent."—*The Times.*

HOWELLS—The Lady of the Aroostook.

2 Vols. 2s.

"There are few more perfect stories than *The Lady of the Aroostook.*"—*The Times.*

HOWELLS—A Fearful Responsibility and Tonelli's Marriage.

"The great body of the cultivated public has an instinctive delight in original genius, whether it be refined or sensational. Mr. Howells's is eminently refined. His humour, however vivid in form, is subtle and elusive in its essence. He depends, perhaps, somewhat too much on the feeling of humour in his readers to appreciate his own."—E. P. WHIPPLE.

HOWELLS—The Undiscovered Country.

2 Vols. 2s.

"The story is, like all Mr. Howells's creations, skilfully constructed and wrought out with careful elaboration of detail."—*Freeman.*

HOWELLS—A Counterfeit Presentment, a Comedy, and a Parlour Car, a Farce.

"In this comedy Mr. Howells gives new proof of his rare insight into character, and ability to portray it by effective and discriminating touches, of his fine sense of dramatic scenes and incidents, and of his exquisite literary skill."

HOWELLS—Out of the Question, a Comedy, and At the Sign of the Savage.

"We may safely prophesy that among the cultivated class of readers Mr. Howells's books will be in steady demand. There are already six or seven of them issued in a cheap form by the publisher of *A Modern Instance.* From our own knowledge we can recommend *A Chance Acquaintance* and *The Undiscovered Country* as books of careful workmanship and accurate observation, written from the American point of view, and without the least apparent influence, either in style or point of view, of English writers.—*Saturday Review.*

HOWELLS—Novels.

These 10 vols., neatly bound in cloth gilt, in box, 21s.

HOWELLS—Venetian Life. 2 Vols.

"His faculties of shrewd, sympathetic observation possessed itself easily of Italian sights and characters, but through all the track of Venetian lagoons or Florentine streets one feels the racy American temper, nothing daunted by the Old World. No description of Venice could be, as far as they go, more daintily, affectionately true."—*Times.*

HOWELLS—Italian Journeys. 2 Vols.

"*Venetian Life* and *Italian Journeys* are delightful reading, and they bear the promise of the future novelist in them. When he travelled in Italian towns he was studying human nature, and fortunately there have been preserved in these two books a vast number of little studies, minute observations, such as in abundance go to make the writer of fiction."—*Century.* [*In the Press.*

IRVING—A Memorial Sketch and a Selection from the Letters of the late Lieut. John Irving, R.N., of H.M.S. "Terror," in Sir John Franklin's Expedition to the Arctic Regions. Edited by Benjamin Bell, F.R.C.S.E. With Facsimiles of the Record and Irving's Medal and Map. 1 vol. post 8vo, 5s.

Jack and Mrs. Brown, and other Stories.

By the Author of "Blindpits." 1 vol. crown 8vo. [*In the Press.*

JENKIN—Healthy Houses.

By Fleeming Jenkin, F.R.S., Professor of Engineering in the University of Edinburgh. Demy 8vo, 2s. 6d.

"The three lectures will be found specially useful to the largely increasing class of house proprietors."—*Courant.*

JERVISE—Epitaphs and Inscriptions from Burial-Grounds and Old Buildings in the North-East of Scotland. By the late Andrew Jervise, F.S.A. Scot. With a Memoir of the Author. Vol. II. Cloth, small 4to, 32s.

Do do. Roxburghe Edition, 42s.

JERVISE—The History and Traditions of the Land of the Lindsays in Angus and Mearns. New Edition, Edited and Revised by the Rev. JAMES GAMMACK. In 1 vol. demy 8vo. 14s.

Do. do. Large Paper Edition [of which only 50 are printed], demy 4to, Roxburghe binding, 42s.

"The editing of these remains has been very careful, and the book, though it has its arid tracts, is sure to please *north country readers.*"

JOASS—A Brief Review of the Silver Question, 1871 to 1879. By EDWARD C. JOASS, Fellow of the Faculty of Actuaries, Edin. 8vo, 1s.

KENNEDY—Pilate's Question, "Whence art Thou?" An Essay on the Personal Claims asserted by Jesus Christ, and how to account for them. By JOHN KENNEDY, M.A., D.D., London. Crown 8vo, 3s. 6d.

"Written on a skilfully arranged plan, is unquestionably a powerful and eloquent vindication of the orthodox and Catholic belief in opposition to rationalistic theories."—*Scotsman.*

KER—Sermons by the Rev. John Ker, D.D., Glasgow. Twelfth Edition. Crown 8vo, 6s.

"A very remarkable volume of sermons."—*Contemporary Review.*

"The sermons before us are of no common order; among a host of competitors they occupy a high class—we were about to say the highest class—whether viewed in point of composition, or thought, or treatment."—*B. and F. Evangelical Review.*

KNIGHT—The English Lake District as interpreted in the Poems of Wordsworth. By WILLIAM KNIGHT, Professor of Moral Philosophy in the University of St. Andrews. Ex. fcap. 8vo, 5s.

KNIGHT—Colloquia Peripatetica (Deep Sea Soundings); Being Notes of Conversations with the late John Duncan, LL.D., Professor of Hebrew in the New College, Edinburgh. By WILLIAM KNIGHT, Professor of Moral Philosophy in the University of St. Andrews. Fifth Edition, enlarged. 5s.

"Since these lectures were published there has appeared an exceedingly interesting volume entitled 'Colloquia Peripatetica,' by the late John Duncan, LL.D., Professor of Hebrew in the New College, Edinburgh. These Colloquies are reported by the Rev. Wm. Knight, who seems to be admirably adapted for the task he has undertaken. His friend must have been a man of rare originality, varied culture, great vigour in expressing thoughts which were worthy to be expressed and remembered. . . . The reader who shall give himself the benefit and gratification of studying this short volume (it will suggest more to him than many of ten times its size) will find that I have not been bribed to speak well of it by any praise which Dr. Duncan has bestowed on me. The only excuse for alluding to it is, that it contains the severest censure on my writings which they have ever incurred, though they have not been so unfortunate as to escape censure. . . . Against any ordinary criticism, even a writer who is naturally thin-skinned becomes by degrees tolerably hardened. One proceeding from a man of such learning and worth as Dr. Duncan I have thought it a duty to notice."—*Extract from Preface to "The Conscience." By the late Professor F. D. Maurice, Second Edition*, 1872.

LAING—Lindores Abbey, and the Burgh of Newburgh; Their History and Annals. By ALEXANDER LAING, LL.D., F.S.A. Scot. 1 vol. small 4to. With Index, and thirteen Full-page and ten Woodcut Illustrations, 21s.

"This is a charming volume in every respect."—*Notes and Queries.*

"The prominent characteristics of the work are its exhaustiveness and the thoroughly philosophic spirit in which it is written."—*Scotsman.*

LANMAN—Recollections of Curious Characters and Pleasant Places. By CHARLES LANMAN, Washington; Author of "Adventures in the Wilds of America," "A Canoe Voyage up the Mississippi," "A Tour to the River Saguenay," etc. etc. In 1 vol. small demy 8vo, 12s.

The Wizard of Anticosti.
Forest Recollections.
The Hunters of the Sea Elephant.
Around Cape Horn.
Montank Point.
Salmon-Fishing on the Jacques Cartier.
The Boy-Hunter of Chicoutimie.
The Potomac Fisherman.
Sword-Fish Fishing.
Newfoundland.
Block Island, etc.

"It is not unpleasant to be sometimes reminded by the appearance of a book of travel, written with greater fidelity and wider knowledge than is nsually found, how little we know of the world and how large it really is. Mr. Lanman conscientiously notes down all that he has seen and what he knows."—*Saturday Review.*

"A bundle of delightfnl reminiscences touched with that light and graceful hand which is common to all his type."—*Academy.*

LANCASTER—Essays and Reviews.

By the late HENRY H. LANCASTER, Advocate; with a Prefatory Notice by the Rev. B. JOWETT, Master of Balliol College, Oxford. Demy 8vo, with Portrait, 14s.

LAURIE—On the Philosophy of Ethics. An Analytical Essay. By S. S. LAURIE, A.M., F.R.S.E., Professor of the Theory, History, and Practice of Education in the University of Edinburgh. Demy 8vo, 6s.

"Mr. Laurie's volume now before us is in substance, though not in form, a reply to Mr. Mill's Utilitarianism. Mr. Laurie has the metaphysical head and the metaphysical training of his countrymen, and has brought both to bear with great force on the problem proposed."—*Saturday Review.*

LAURIE—Notes on British Theories of Morals.

Demy 8vo, 6s.

"His criticisms are candid and highly instructive, *e.g.* those of the views of Bentham, Mill, and Bain. He manifests great aptitude in detecting radical defects, in exposing logical inconsistencies, and in detecting the legitimate tendencies of philosophical systems."—*British Quarterly.*

LORIMER—Bible Studies in Life and Truth.

By the Rev. ROBERT LORIMER, M.A., Free Church, Mains and Strathmartine In 1 vol. crown 8vo, 5s.

"It is in several respects a remarkable volume. . . These discourses, the outcome of a thoughtful, earnest, and vigorons mind, are written in a strain of chaste and manly eloquence, and they are even more valuable for what they suggest than for what they directly teach."—*Scotsman.*

"There is in these studies much that will help to govern the will, satisfy the mind with truth, and the heart with life."—*Daily Review.*

"The distinctive fragrance of the old evangelical preaching of our fathers is combined with the modern spirit of exact research in Biblical science . . . and these studies may be regarded as a proof that the reconciliation between the old and the new in our Scottish Christian life is not so difficult as some suppose."—*Aberdeen Free Press.*

"On every line of these sermons there is a trace of care and anxious thought. This preacher is no extempore orator. He is a student, and has made himself familiar with the best models."—*Dundee Advertiser.*

"They are characterised by penetrative thought, lucidity, and cogency of statement, and a chaste and classic eloquence. They evince earnest study and wide reading."—*Glasgow Herald.*

LIND—Sermons.

By Rev. Adam Lind, M.A., Elgin. Ex. fcap. 8vo, 5s.

A Lost Battle.

A Novel. 2 vols. Crown 8vo, 17s.

"This in every way remarkable novel."—*Morning Post.*

"We are all the more ready to do justice to the excellence of the author's drawing of characters."—*Athenæum.*

M'CRIE—John Calvin, a Fragment by the Late Thomas M'Crie, Author of "The Life of John Knox." Demy 8vo, 6s.

MACFARLANE—Principles of the Algebra of Logic, with Examples, by Alex. MacFarlane, M.A., D.Sc. (Edin.), F.R.S.E. 5s.

MACKAY—Memoir of Sir James Dalrymple, First Viscount Stair. A Study in the History of Scotland and Scotch Law during the Seventeenth Century. By Æ. J. G. Mackay, Advocate. 8vo, 12s.

MACLAGAN—Nugæ Canoræ Medicæ.

Lays of the Poet Laureate of the New Town Dispensary. Edited by Professor Douglas Maclagan. 4to. With Illustrations, 7s. 6d.

MACLAGAN—The Hill Forts, Stone Circles, and other Structural Remains of Ancient Scotland. By C. Maclagan, Lady Associate of the Society of Antiquaries of Scotland. With Plans and Illustrations. 1 vol. fol., 31s. 6d.

"We need not enlarge on the few inconsequential speculations which rigid archæologists may find in the present volume. We desire rather to commend it to their careful study, fully assured that not only they, but also the general reader, will be edified by its perusal."—*Scotsman.*

M'LAREN—The Light of the World.

By David M'Laren, Minister of Humbie. Crown 8vo, extra, 6s.

"We are conscious of having but very inadequately represented this valuable book, and can only hope that what we have said may lead all who have the opportunity to study it for themselves."—*Literary World.*

MACPHERSON—Omnipotence belongs only to the Beloved.

By Mrs. Brewster Macpherson. 1 vol. extra fcap., 3s. 6d.

MAXWELL—Antwerp Delivered in MDLXXVII.;

A Passage from the History of the Netherlands, illustrated with Facsimiles of a rare Series of Designs by Martin de Vos, and of Prints by Hogenberg, the Wierixes, etc. By Sir William Stirling-Maxwell, Bart., K.T. and M.P. In 1 vol. folio, 5 guineas.

"A splendid folio in richly ornamented binding, protected by an almost equally ornamental slip-cover. . . . Remarkable illustrations of the manner in which the artists of the time 'pursued their labours in a country ravaged by war, and in cities ever menaced by siege and sack.'"—*Scotsman.*

MICHIE—History of Loch Kinnord.

By the Rev. J. G. Michie. Demy 8vo, 2s. 6d.

"It is throughout a piece of genuine, honest, literary workmanship, dealing thoroughly with its subject on the basis of careful study and personal inquiry and labour."—*Aberdeen Free Press.*

MILN—Researches and Excavations at Carnac (Morbihan),
The Bossenno, and Mont St. Michel. By JAMES MILN. In 1 vol. royal 8vo, with Maps, Plans, and numerous Illustrations in Wood-Engraving and Chromolithography.

"Mr. Miln has made some interesting discoveries, and his record of them is simply and modestly written. He seems to have spared no pains either in making his excavations, or in writing and illustrating an account of them. . . . Mr. Miln has thus an opportunity worthy of an ambitious archæologist, and he has succeeded in using it well."—*Saturday Review.*

"This elegant volume, one of those which are the luxury of art, is the work of an enthusiastic and well-informed antiquary."—*British Quarterly.*

MILN—Excavations at Carnac (Brittany), a Record of Archæ-ological Researches in the Alignments of Kermario. By JAMES MILN. In 1 vol. royal 8vo, with Maps, Plans, and numerous Illustrations in Wood-Engraving. 15s.

MITCHELL—The Past in the Present—What is Civilisa-tion? Being the Rhind Lectures in Archæology, delivered in 1876 and 1878. By ARTHUR MITCHELL, M.D., LL.D., Secretary to the Society of Antiquaries of Scotland. In 1 vol. demy 8vo, with 148 Woodcuts, 15s.

"Whatever differences of opinion, however, may be held on minor points, there can be no question that Dr. Mitchell's work is one of the ablest and most original pieces of archæological literature which has appeared of late years."—*St. James's Gazette.*

MITCHELL—Our Scotch Banks:
Their Position and their Policy. By WM. MITCHELL, S.S.C. Third Edition. 8vo, 5s.

MOLBECH—Ambrosius:
A Play, translated from the Danish of Christian K. F. Molbech by ALICE BERRY. Extra fcap. 8vo, 5s.

MORETON—On Horse-Breaking.
By ROBERT MORETON. Second Edition. [*In the Press.*

MUIR—Ecclesiological Notes on some of the Islands of Scotland, with other Papers relating to Ecclesiological Remains on the Scottish Mainland and Islands. By THOMAS S. MUIR, author of "Characteristics of Church Architecture," etc. In 1 vol. demy 8vo, with numerous Illustrations. [*In Preparation.*

MUNRO—Ancient Scottish Lake-Dwellings or Crannogs, with a Supplementary Chapter on Remains of Lake-Dwellings in England. By ROBERT MUNRO, M.D., F.S.A. Scot. 1 vol. demy 8vo, profusely illustrated, price 21s.

"It is a most valuable and methodical statement of all the facts connected with his own excavations in Ayrshire. It will doubtless become a standard authority on the subject of which it treats."—*Times.*

". . . Our readers may be assured that they will find very much to interest and instruct them in the perusal of the work."—*Athenæum.*

". . . The issue of these reports in a handy volume was taken in hand by Dr. Munro, and the result is seen in the carefully-prepared and admirably got-up volume to which we have now to invite attention."—*Saturday Review.*

NAPIER—"The Lanox of Auld:"
An Epistolary Review of "The Lennox, by William Fraser." By MARK NAPIER. With Woodcuts and Plates. 1 vol. 4to, 15s.

"The spirit of chivalry survives, though the age is gone. If any one doubts it he has only to dip into the pages of 'Lanox of Auld.' . . . It places the reader in possession of both sides of the questions relating to the 'Earldom of Lennox.'"—*Scotsman.*

NICHOLSON—Tenants' Gain not Landlords' Loss, and some other Economic Aspects of the Land Question. By JOSEPH SHIELD NICHOLSON, M.A., Professor of Political Economy in the University of Edinburgh. 1 vol. crown 8vo. [*In the Press.*

OBER—Camps in the Caribbees: Adventures of a Naturalist in the Lesser Antilles. By FREDERICK OBER. Illustrations, sm. 8vo, 12s.

"Well-written and well-illustrated narrative of camping out among the Caribbees."—*Westminster Review.*

"Varied were his experiences, hairbreadth his escapes, and wonderful his gleanings in the way of securing rare birds."—*The Literary World.*

OGG—Cookery for the Sick and a Guide for the Sick-Room. By C. H. OGG, an Edinburgh Nurse. Fcap. 1s.

OMOND—The Lord Advocates of Scotland from the close of the Fifteenth Century to the passing of the Reform Bill. By G. W. T. OMOND, Advocate. 2 vols. demy 8vo. 28s.

PATRICK, R. W. COCHRAN—Records of the Coinage of Scotland, from the earliest period to the Union. Collected by R. W. COCHRAN-PATRICK, M.P. Only two hundred and fifty copies printed. Now ready, in 2 vols. 4to, with 16 Full-page Illustrations, Six Guineas.

"The future Historians of Scotland will be very fortunate if many parts of their materials are so carefully worked up for them and set before them in so complete and taking a form."—*Athenæum.*

"When we say that these two volumes contain more than 770 records, of which more than 550 have never been printed before, and that they are illustrated by a series of Plates, by the autotype process, of the coins themselves, the reader may judge for himself of the learning, as well as the pains, bestowed on them both by the Author and the Publisher."—*Times.*

"The most handsome and complete Work of the kind which has ever been published in this country."—*Numismatic Chronicle, Pt. IV.*, 1876.

"We have in these Records of the Coinage of Scotland, not the production of a *dilettante*, but of a real student, who, with rare pains and the most scholarly diligence, has set to work and collected into two massive volumes a complete history of the coinage of Scotland, so far as it can be gathered from the ancient records." —*Academy.*

PATRICK—Early Records relating to Mining in Scotland: Collected by R. W. COCHRAN-PATRICK, M.P. Demy 4to, 31s. 6d.

"The documents contained in the body of the work are given without alteration or abridgment, and the introduction is written with ability and judgment, presenting a clear and concise outline of the earlier history of the Mining Industries of Scotland."—*Scotsman.*

"The documents . . . comprise a great deal that is very curious, and no less that will be important to the historian in treating of the origin of one of the most important branches of the national industry."—*Daily News.*

"Such a book . . . revealing as it does the first developments of an industry which has become the mainspring of the national prosperity, ought to be specially interesting to all patriotic Scotchmen."—*Saturday Review.*

PATRICK—The Medals of Scotland: a Descriptive Catalogue of the Royal and other Medals relating to Scotland. By R. W. COCHRAN-PATRICK, M.P., of Woodside. Dedicated by special permission to Her Majesty the Queen. In 1 vol. 4to, with plates in facsimile of all the principal pieces. [*In the Press*

Popular Genealogists;

Or, The Art of Pedigree-making. Crown 8vo, 4s.

"We have here an agreeable little treatise of a hundred pages, from an anonymous but evidently competent hand, on the ludicrous and fraudulent sides of genealogy. The subject has a serious and important historical character, when regarded from the point of view of the authors of *The Governing Families of England.* But it is rich in the materials of comedy also.

"The first case selected by the writer before us is one which has often excited our mirth by the very completeness of its unrivalled absurdity. Nobody can turn over the popular genealogical books of our day without dropping on a family called Coulthart of Coulthart, Collyn, and Ashton-under-Lyne. The pedigree given makes the house beyond all question the oldest in Europe. Neither the Bourbons nor Her Majesty's family can be satisfactorily carried beyond the ninth century, whereas the Coultharts were by that time an old and distinguished house.

"We are glad to see such a step taken in the good work as the publication of the essay which has suggested this article, and which we commend to those who want a bit of instructive and amusing reading."—*Pall Mall Gazette.*

PORTER—The Gamekeeper's Manual: being Epitome of the

Game Laws for the use of Gamekeepers and others interested in the Preservation of Game. By ALEXANDER PORTER, Deputy Chief Constable of Roxburghshire. Fcap. 8vo, 1s.

REID—Pictures from the Orkney Islands.

By JOHN T. REID, Author of "Art Rambles in Shetland." In 1 vol. 4to, with numerous Illustrations, 25s.

RENTON, W.—Oils and Water Colours.

By WILLIAM RENTON. 1 vol. fcap., 5s.

"The book is obviously for the Artist and the Poet, and for every one who shares with them a true love and zeal for nature's beauties."—*Scotsman.*

"To have observed such a delicate bit of colouring as this, and to have written so good a sonnet in the 'strict style,' as that we have quoted, shows that our author has no common powers either as an observer or a writer."—*Liverpool Albion.*

"To those minds that really hold this joy in beauty, Mr. Renton's book will undoubtedly give delight."—*Northern Ensign.*

ROBERTSON—Kuram, Kabul, and Kandahar: being a Brief

Record of the Impressions in Three Campaigns under General Roberts. By Lieut. ROBERTSON, 8th, "The King's," Regiment. 1 vol. crown 8vo, with Maps, 6s.

ROBERTSON—Historical Essays,

In connection with the Land and the Church, etc. By E. WILLIAM ROBERTSON, Author of "Scotland under her Early Kings." In 1 vol. 8vo, 10s. 6d.

ROBERTSON—Scotland under her Early Kings.

A History of the Kingdom to the close of the 13th century. By E. WILLIAM ROBERTSON. In 2 vols. 8vo, cloth, 36s.

"Mr. Robertson's labours are of that valuable kind where an intelligent and thorough sifting of original authorities is brought to bear upon a portion of history handed over hitherto, in a pre-eminent degree, to a specially mendacious set of Mediæval Chroniclers, and (not so long ago) to a specially polemical and uncritical class of modern historians. He belongs to the school of Innes and Skene and Joseph Robertson, and has established a fair right to be classed with the Reeves and Todds of Irish historical antiquarianism, and the Sharpes, and Kembles, and Hardys in England."—*Guardian.*

ROSEBERY—A Rectorial Address Delivered before the Students of Aberdeen University, in the Music Hall at Aberdeen, on Nov. 5, 1880. By Lord Rosebery. In demy 8vo, price 6d.

ROSEBERY—A Rectorial Address delivered before the Students of the University of Edinburgh, November 4, 1882. By Lord Rosebery. Demy 8vo, price 6d.

ST. JOHN—Notes and Sketches from the Wild Coasts of Nipon. With Chapters on Cruising after Pirates in Chinese Waters. By Henry C. St. John, Captain R.N. In 1 vol. small demy 8vo, with Maps and Illustrations, price 12s.

Round Yesso.
The Inland Sea Revisited.
Currents and Typhoons.
A Summer's Walk in Kiusiu.
Deer-Shooting and other matters.
The Kii Coast.
Insects.
Shooting, etc.
Singing-Birds and Flowers, etc.
Customs and Habits.
Past and Present.
Korea.
Cruising after Pirates.
Shooting in China.
More Cruising after Pirates.
Résumé.

"One of the most charming books of travel that has been published for some time."—*Scotsman.*

"There is a great deal more in the book than Natural History. . . . His pictures of life and manners are quaint and effective, and the more so from the writing being natural and free from effort."—*Athenæum.*

"He writes with a simplicity and directness, and not seldom with a degree of graphic power, which, even apart from the freshness of the matter, render his book delightful reading. Nothing could be better of its kind than the description of the inland sea."—*Daily News.*

"He dedicates the volume in a few graceful sentences to the memory of his father, the well-known author of the 'Wild Sports and Natural History of the Highlands,' &c. The son has certainly inherited the father's love of sport. . . . Written in a perfectly simple and unpretending style, it bears evidence of much literary taste, and is eminently the work of a keen sportsman."—*Aberdeen Free Press.*

"The notes of so keen an observer of the habits of plants, insects, and animals, and on sea currents and storms, are not merely of curious interest in themselves, they will be of the highest value in illustrating the natural history and meteorology of a region which, from its situation and productions, is of singular interest to science."—*Scotsman.*

"Clearly and tersely written, obviously the product of personal observation by one who is primarily a lover and observer of nature."—*Inverness Courier.*

"For seven years he was surveying in Japan, and this work is the fruit of his winter leisure. While coasting round Yesso and the Kuriles he constantly kept the dredge at work, and discovered many new creatures. He does not confine himself to natural history; he tells us a great deal more than even Miss Bird of life in the interior of Japan. The book will take high rank."—*Graphic.*

"His rough notes of their very primitive ways are pleasantly put together—some of these 'ways' being extremely 'peculiar,' according to European ideas, but with a strange mixture of good and evil. Supporters of foreign missions might do worse than study Captain St. John's remarks on the difference between the progress of Roman Catholic and Protestant missionary enterprise in the far East."—*North British Daily Mail.*

ST. JOHN—Notes on the Natural History of the Province

of Moray. By the late CHARLES ST. JOHN, author of "Wild Sports in the Highlands." Second Edition. In 1 vol. royal 8vo, with 40 page Illustrations of Scenery and Animal Life, engraved by A. DURAND after sketches made by GEORGE REID, R.S.A., and J. WYCLIFFE TAYLOR; also, 30 Pen-and-ink Drawings by the author in facsimile. Price 50s.

"This is a new edition of the work brought out by the friends of the late Mr. St. John in 1863; but it is so handsomely and nobly printed, and enriched with such charming illustrations, that we may consider it a new book."—*St. James's Gazette.*

"Charles St. John was not an artist, but he had the habit of roughly sketching animals in positions which interested him, and the present reprint is adorned by a great number of these, facsimiled from the author's original pen and ink. Some of these, as, for instance, the studies of the golden eagle swooping on its prey, and that of the otter swimming with a salmon in its mouth, are very interesting, and full of that charm that comes from the exact transcription of unusual observation."—*Pall Mall Gazette.*

"The feature of the present edition is the series of beautiful sketches made specially for this volume by Mr. George Reid, R.S.A., and Mr. Wycliffe Taylor together with numberless pieces from St. John's own sketch-book introduced into the text. 'Roughness' they (the latter) certainly possess, almost as if St. John had thrown the inkstand at the paper, but withal a spirit of suggestiveness which makes them well-nigh unique among portraits of birds and other animals, and we cannot be too grateful to the editor for presenting them in this form."—*Nation (New York).*

SCHIERN—Life of James Hepburn, Earl of Bothwell.

By Professor SCHIERN, Copenhagen. Translated from the Danish by the Rev. DAVID BERRY, F.S.A. Scot. Demy 8vo, 16s.

"The real interest in the book lies in the information which it contains about the life of Bothwell after the surrender at Carberry. The only trustworthy information concerning the latter period of his life must be sought from Scandinavian sources."

"Not only well written and interesting, but at the same time so thoroughly trustworthy that it can well bear the test of close critical examination."—*Saturday Review.*

Scotch Folk.

Illustrated. Third Edition enlarged. Ex. fcap. 8vo, price 1s.

"They are stories of the best type, quite equal in the main to the average of Dean Ramsay's well-known collection."—*Aberdeen Free Press.*

SHAIRP—Studies in Poetry and Philosophy.

By J. C. SHAIRP, LL.D., Principal of the United College of St. Salvator and St. Leonard, St. Andrews. Second Edition. 1 vol. fcap. 8vo, 6s.

"In the 'Moral Dynamic,' Mr. Shairp seeks for something which shall persuade us of the vital and close bearing on each other of moral thought and spiritual energy. It is this conviction which has animated Mr. Shairp in every page of the volume before us. It is because he appreciates so justly and forcibly the powers of philosophic doctrine over all the field of human life, that he leans with such strenuous trust upon those ideas which Wordsworth unsystematically, and Coleridge more systematically, made popular and fertile among us."—*Saturday Review.*

"The finest essay in the volume, partly because it is upon the greatest and most definite subject, is the first, on *Wordsworth*. . . . We have said so much upon this essay that we can only say of the other three that they are fully worthy to stand beside it."—*Spectator.*

SHAIRP—Culture and Religion.

By Principal Shairp, LL.D. Fifth Edition. Fcap. 8vo, 3s. 6d.

"A wise book, and unlike a great many other wise books, has that carefully shaded thought and expression which fits Professor Shairp to speak for Culture no less than for Religion."—*Spectator.*

"Those who remember a former work of Principal Shairp's, 'Studies in Poetry and Philosophy,' will feel secure that all which comes from his pen will bear the marks of thought, at once careful, liberal, and accurate. Nor will they be disappointed in the present work. . . . We can recommend this book to our readers."—*Athenæum.*

"We cannot close without earnestly recommending the book to thoughtful young men. They will find in it the work of a cultivated and learned mind, and of a pure, generous, and upright heart. It combines the loftiest intellectual power with a simple and childlike faith in Christ, and exerts an influence which must be stimulating and healthful."—*Freeman.*

SHAIRP—On Poetic Interpretation of Nature.

By J. C. Shairp, LL.D., Principal of the United College of St. Salvator and St. Leonard, St. Andrews. Second Edition. In 1 vol. ex. fcap. 8vo, 6s.

"There is a real sense of relief and refreshment on turning from the news of the day to the unspeakable repose of nature, and in the sense of coolness, and stillness, and greenness, of which we become conscious as we follow Professor Shairp through these interesting and suggestive pages."—*Times.*

SHAIRP—Wordsworth's Tour in Scotland in 1803, in Company with his Sister and S. T. Coleridge;

being the Journal of Miss Wordsworth, now for the first time made public. Edited by Principal Shairp, LL.D. Second Edition. 1 vol. crown 8vo, 6s.

"If there were no other record of her than those brief extracts from Her Journal during the Highland Tour, which stand at the head of several of her brother's poems, these alone would prove her possessed of a large portion of his genius."—*North British Review.*

"The volume glistens with passages nearly as charming, showing how rich in 'Wordsworthian' fancy, was this modest sister. . . . We have to thank Dr. Shairp, and the thanks must be hearty, for now for the first time giving them in a complete form."—*Athenæum.*

"All who love Wordsworth and Nature will welcome this book. To many it will add a more precious seeing to the eye, and make them understand how, if they look, they will see."—*Scotsman.*

"Next to the charming simplicity we like the quiet, picturesque power of this diary."—*Dundee Advertiser.*

"The book is one to be read and prized—to be read through with delight, and to be often taken up again with an over full enjoyment."—*Daily Review.*

"A simple, and in many respects a touching record is this, brimming over with sisterly love—womanly, tender, and graceful."—*Standard.*

"Many readers will turn with a pure delight from mental wars and questions to wander amid the grandeur and beauty of Scottish glens and mountains in the company of so bright a being as Dora Wordsworth, the loved and loving sister of the poet.—*Windsor Gazette.*

"As a picture of Scotland seventy years ago, there is not in the whole compass of English Literature a work that can be said to equal or even approach this one."—*Literary World.*

"The 'Journal' would be worth reading if it were only for the sake of finding these lines in their proper place. '*What? you are stepping Westward? Yea.*'"—*Academy.*

"It will extend the fame of Wordsworth, and cause many who know him not, or are little acquainted with his writings, to become his admirers; and evermore with us the name 'Dorothy' shall be melodious as the name of one who is a sweet-souled benefactress of our race."—*Aberdeen Herald.*

SHAIRP—Kilmahoe, a Highland Pastoral,

And other Poems. Fcap. 8vo, 6s.

SIMPSON—The Near and the Far View,

And other Sermons. By Rev. A. L. SIMPSON, D.D., Derby. 1 vol. ex. fcap. 8vo, 5s.

"Very fresh and thoughtful are these sermons."—*Literary World.*

"Dr. Simpson's sermons may fairly claim distinctive power. He looks at things with his own eyes, and often shows us what with ordinary vision we had failed to perceive. . . . The sermons are distinctively good."—*British Quarterly Review.*

SIMPSON—Archæological Essays.

By the late Sir JAMES SIMPSON, Bart. Edited by the late JOHN STUART, LL.D. 2 vols. 4to, 21s.

1. Archæology.
2. Inchcolm.
3. The Cat Stane.
4. Magical Charm-Stones.
5. Pyramid of Gizeh.
6. Leprosy and Leper Hospitals.
7. Greek Medical Vases.
8. Was the Roman Army provided with Medical Officers?
9. Roman Medicine Stamps, [etc. etc.

SKENE—The Four Ancient Books of Wales,

Containing the Cymric Poems attributed to the Bards of the sixth century. By WILLIAM F. SKENE, Historiographer-Royal for Scotland. With Maps and Facsimiles. 2 vols. 8vo, 36s.

"Mr. Skene's book will, as a matter of course and necessity, find its place on the tables of all Celtic antiquarians and scholars."—*Archæologia Cambrensis.*

SKENE—Celtic Scotland: A History of Ancient Alban.

In Three vols. 45s. Illustrated with Maps.

I.—HISTORY and ETHNOLOGY. II.—CHURCH and CULTURE.
III.—LAND and PEOPLE.

"Forty years ago Mr. Skene published a small historical work on the Scottish Highlands which has ever since been appealed to as an authority, but which has long been out of print. The promise of this youthful effort is amply fulfilled in the three weighty volumes of his maturer years. As a work of historical research it ought in our opinion to take a very high rank."—*Times.*

SMALL—Scottish Woodwork of the Sixteenth and Seventeenth Centuries. Measured, Drawn, and Lithographed by J. W. SMALL, Architect. In one folio volume, with 130 Plates, Four Guineas.

"Mr. J. W. Small's very admirable volume, illustrative of ancient Scottish woodwork. . . . It is impossible to over-estimate the value of the minute details that abound in Mr. Small's admirable work. Very opportunely has Mr. Small come to the rescue of art furniture with his admirable work, of which it is impossible to speak in unduly eulogistic terms."—*Furniture Gazette.*

SMITH—Shelley: a Critical Biography.

By GEORGE BARNETT SMITH. Ex. fcap. 8vo, 6s.

SMITH—The Sermon on the Mount.

By the Rev. WALTER C. SMITH, D.D. Crown 8vo, 6s.

SMITH—Answer to the Form of Libel before the Free Presbytery of Aberdeen. By W. ROBERTSON SMITH, Professor of Oriental Languages and Exegesis of the Old Testament in the Free Church College, Aberdeen. 8vo, 1s.

SMITH—Additional Answer to the Libel,

With some Account of the Evidence that parts of the Pentateuchal Law are later than the Time of Moses. By W. ROBERTSON SMITH, Professor of Oriental Languages and Exegesis of the Old Testament in the Free Church College, Aberdeen. 8vo, 1s.

SMITH—Answer to the Amended Libel, with Appendix

containing Plea in Law. By W. ROBERTSON SMITH. 8vo, 6d.

SMITH—Open Letter to Principal Rainy. 6d.

SMYTH—Life and Work at the Great Pyramid.

With a Discussion of the Facts ascertained. By C. PIAZZI SMYTH, F.R.SS.L. and E., Astronomer-Royal for Scotland. 3 vols. demy 8vo, 56s.

SMYTH—Madeira: Meteorologic.

Being a Paper on the above subject read before the Royal Society, Edinburgh, on the 1st of May 1882. By C. PIAZZI SMYTH, Astronomer-Royal for Scotland. In 1 vol. small 4to, price 6s.

SOUTHESK—Saskatchewan and the Rocky Mountains.

Diary and Narrative of Travel, Sport, and Adventure, during a Journey through part of the Hudson's Bay Company's Territories in 1859 and 1860. By the EARL OF SOUTHESK, K.T., F.R.G.S. 1 vol. demy 8vo, with Illustrations on Wood by WHYMPER, 18s.

SOUTHESK—Herminius.

A Romance. By I. E. S. Fcap. 8vo, 6s.

SOUTHESK—Jonas Fisher.

A Poem in Brown and White. Cheap Edition. Price 1s.

SPEDDING. See GAIRDNER.

SPENS—Darroll, and other Poems.

By WALTER COOK SPENS, Advocate. Crown 8vo, 5s.

"This volume will repay perusal. It is one which could have been written only by a man of culture."—*Daily Review.*

"He writes with feeling, and displays considerable facility in the handling of almost every ordinary variety of metre."—*Scotsman.*

SPENS—Should the Poor-Law in all Cases Deny Relief to

the Able-bodied Poor? By WALTER COOK SPENS, Advocate, Sheriff-Substitute of Lanarkshire. Demy 8vo, 1s.

SPINNAKER—Spindrift from the Hebrides.

By SPINNAKER. With Eight Etchings. Crown 8vo, 1s. 6d.

STOCKTON—Rudder Grange.

By FRANK R. STOCKTON. 1 vol. 1s., and cloth 2s.

STEVENSON—Christianity Confirmed by Jewish and Heathen Testimony, and the Deductions from Physical Science, etc. By THOMAS STEVENSON, F.R.S.E., F.G.S., Member of the Institution of Civil Engineers. Second Edition. Fcap. 8vo, 3s. 6d.

STRACHAN—What is Play?

A Physiological Inquiry. Its bearing upon Education and Training. By JOHN STRACHAN, M.D., Jun. In 1 vol. fcap., 1s.

"We have great pleasure in directing the attention of our readers to this little work . . . bearing as it does on one of the most important aspects of physiological medicine, as well as on education in the highest sense of the word."—*Lancet.*

"A very interesting, and, in the main, a wise little book."—*Mind.*

"It is so seldom that so much sound sense, clear reasoning, and able development of ideas, which will probably be new to the majority of readers, are compressed into a hundred duodecimo pages, as Dr. Strachan has contrived to put into his little treatise *on Play.*"—*Scotsman.*

TAIT—Sketch of Thermodynamics.

By P. G. TAIT, Professor of Natural Philosophy in the University of Edinburgh. Second Edition, revised and extended. Crown 8vo, 5s.

Talks with our Farm-Servants.

By An Old Farm-Servant. Crown 8vo; paper 6d., cloth 1s.

Tommie Brown and the Queen of the Fairies; a new Child's Book, in fcap. 8vo. With Illustrations, 4s. 6d.

Let pain be pleasure, and pleasure be pain.

"There is no wonder that children liked the story. It is told neatly and well, and is full of great cleverness, while it has that peculiar character the absence of which from many like stories deprives them of any real interest for children."—*Scotsman.*

"The story is a delightful bit of fancy, primarily calculated to create wonderment in the youthful mind, but none but the dullest reader will turn over the pages of the engrossing narrative without discovering that the author inculcates numerous lessons of the most wholesome kind."—*Daily Review.*

"The author has contributed a story which could not fail to delight the hearts of fairy-tale loving children."—*Aberdeen Free Press.*

TROTTER—Our Mission to the Court of Marocco in 1880, under Sir JOHN DRUMMOND HAY, K.C.B., Minister Plenipotentiary at Tangier, and Envoy Extraordinary to His Majesty the Sultan of Marocco. By Captain PHILIP DURHAM TROTTER, 93d Highlanders. Illustrated from Photographs by the Hon. D. LAWLESS, Rifle Brigade. In 1 vol. square demy 8vo, 24s.

"Very attractively written . . . . not only highly instructive but also extremely amusing."—*Times.*

"We may fairly say that there is an antiquarian flavour about these volumes which Scotchmen will relish, and which Englishmen need not undervalue or despise."—*Saturday Review.*

"There is much in this book which is well worth reading, and the author's style is always lively. The illustrations of the most interesting places and ruins are from photographs taken by Mr. Lawless, and are very successful."—*Guardian.*

The Book-Lover's Enchiridion: a Selection of Thoughts on the Solace and Companionship of Books. Red edges 5s., gilt 6s.

The Upland Tarn: A Village Idyll.
In 1 vol. small crown, price 5s.

WILSON—The Botany of Three Historical Records:
Pharaoh's Dream, The Sower, and the King's Measure. By A. STEPHEN WILSON. Crown 8vo, with 5 plates, 3s. 6d.

"The book is useful as affording illustrations of Scripture incident and teaching."—*Inverness Courier.*

"The writer deserves credit for the pains he has taken in making his researches, and by means of well-designed woodcuts he has so illustrated the work as to make his arguments as clear as is possible."—*Courant.*

WILSON—'A Bushel of Corn.'
By A. STEPHEN WILSON. In 1 vol. crown 8vo. [*In the Press.*

WILSON—Reminiscences of Old Edinburgh.
By DANIEL WILSON, LL.D., F.R.S.E., Professor of History and English Literature in University College, Toronto, Author of "Prehistoric Annals of Scotland," etc. etc. 2 vols. post 8vo, 15s.

WYLD—Christianity and Reason:
Their necessary connection. By R. S. WYLD, LL.D. Extra fcap. 8vo, 3s. 6d.

www.ingramcontent.com/pod-product-compliance
Lightning Source LLC
Chambersburg PA
CBHW030822270326
41928CB00007B/845

* 9 7 8 3 3 3 7 3 1 2 1 0 7 *